TO PREACH THE GOSPEL

Peter Marshall at Saint Andrew's Society Gala
Waldorf Astoria, November 20, 1945

TO PREACH THE GOSPEL

THE ZIMMERMAN LECTURES ON EFFECTIVE PREACHING

The Reverend Dr. Peter Marshall

Senior Pastor, The New York Avenue Presbyterian Church, Washington, D.C. (1937-1949)

Chaplain, United States Senate (1947-1949)

EVERGREEN
— FARM —

TO PREACH THE GOSPEL

The Zimmerman Lectures on Effective Preaching
The Reverend Dr. Peter Marshall
Copyright ©2026 by Marshall-LeSourd, LLC

EVERGREEN
— FARM —

Published by Evergreen Farm Publishing
P.O. Box 77, Lincoln, VA 20160 USA
www.evergreenfarmbooks.com

ISBN: 978-1-956233-45-2   (printed hardback)
ISBN: 978-1-956233-46-9   (printed paperback)
ISBN: 978-1-956233-47-6   (eBook)

Cover and interior design by Larry Taylor Design, Ltd.

Front cover photo by Evans Morgan Lantz, USN (1909-1990). Image digitally colorized. Back cover photo by Joe Covello. Used under license from Black Star Agency.

Ebook production by BB eBooks

Printed in the United States of America
Unless otherwise indicated, Scripture quotations are taken from the King James Version of the Bible.

In Memoriam

Edith Wallis Marshall Roberts (1942–2016)

Edith first envisioned publication of these lectures
and worked determinedly on the project.
She was married to the Rev. Peter John Marshall,
son of Catherine and Peter Marshall.

The Spirit of the Lord is upon
me because He hath
anointed me to preach the
gospel to the poor;
he hath sent me to heal
the brokenhearted, to preach
deliverance to the captives,
and recovering of sight
to the blind, to set at
liberty them that are
bruised.
To preach the acceptable
year of the Lord

Peter Marshall.

— *Luke 4:18* in Peter Marshall's handwriting
Peter and Catherine Marshall Papers,
Library of Congress Manuscript Division

CONTENTS

PREFACE

"Go Forth and Make Disciples"

Peter Jonathan Marshall

The risk of compiling, editing, and publishing a work such as *To Preach The Gospel: The Zimmerman Lectures on Effective Preaching* is that its readers might find it old, antiquated, or even dated. I confess to having been leery of coming to the same conclusion myself: the fear of having to admit that the eighty-year-old insights of my grandfather—known as one of the great pastors and orators of the twentieth century—were no longer relevant to modern Christianity.

What I discovered, however, was quite the opposite. The words literally leap off the page, not with the glorious tonality of that rhythmic Scottish brogue for which Granddad was known, but with line after line of answers to the most profound of questions. What does it truly mean to be a pastor? How, with all the distractions of the modern pulpit, can I continue to make my life about serving others and serving Christ?

The reader will find in these lectures timeless answers, not only for the young seminarian, but in equal measure for the seasoned vocational pastor.

And while his lectures are instructive and inform modern ministry, my earnest prayer is that you will find rest and encouragement as you read. So that we all, as those who went before us, may fight the good fight and work worthy of the call that God has on all our lives ... *to go forth and make disciples of all nations.*

FOREWORD

WALKING WITH PETER MARSHALL

The Honorable Philip Lader

"When it's 3 o'clock in New York, it's still 1938 in London." With a comedienne's turn at social commentary, Bette Midler prompts the question for us: What might be the relevance today – amidst the past century's revolutions in society, advances of technology, and perspectives gone global – of obscure lectures by a Scottish-bred preacher who first rose to the pulpit of Abraham Lincoln's Washington, D.C., church in 1938?

The answer, for me, is deeply personal. And, perhaps, for you, too. That realization crystallized on long days while my feet ached over country roads and bridleways, along plunging cliffs and in desolate moors, around castles, and by churches inspired by John Wesley, but now apparently congregation-less.

Upon assuming his post, this unlikely U.S. Ambassador to the Court of St. James's – for one long weekend each month in 1997-98 and over a summer holiday – walked the length-&-breadth of Great Britain to better understand the United Kingdom and its people. From Land's End, England's southwestern-most point, to John o'Groats, on the northern tip of Scotland, I trod northward in rain, sleet, mist, snow – and under two double rainbows.

What beckoned, however, was not simply the Highlands' summer sunshine and the land of clans and Burns, whisky and haggis. For a fellow long-before moved by the story of Peter Marshall, "Scotland" was more than tartans, the Loch Ness Monster, or St. Andrews; more than a geographic destination. My meandering path there, following a long series of "coincidental paths-crossings" with this Scot, vividly reminds me of the common spiritual roads which all of us pilgrims – whatever our religious traditions, our beliefs or doubts – journey.

In my childhood, Catherine Marshall's biography of her late husband, stricken by a fatal heart attack when only 46, was widely read: the tale of a boy, working in coal mines, who left a poverty-stricken town near Glasgow and became Chaplain of the United States Senate and one of the most revered religious leaders in wartime and post-World War II America.

The 1955 Oscar-nominated film "A Man Called Peter" had illustrated for me how a message can be better conveyed by painting pictures than by a lecture. Years later, "Chariots of Fire" – the Academy Awards' 1981 Best Picture, about the devout Olympic gold-medalist, Eric Liddell, whose principles and Christian ministry in China had inspired his fellow Scot, Peter Marshall – became my most-repeatedly-viewed movie, its theme music still set as my morning alarm.

Laughter-filled holiday gatherings over the four+ decades since my wedding to Catherine's stepdaughter, Linda LeSourd, have inevitably been punctuated by "Peter sagas" shared with the next generation. Throughout her years of service on the ministerial staff of The New York Avenue Presbyterian Church, where Dr. Marshall had been named pastor at the age of 35, Sunday-morning worshipers from across the country, unaware of her personal link, would regularly inquire about Peter Marshall.

That historic church occupies a unique place in the country's history, even more significant than its location steps from the White House. In 1861 and throughout the Civil War, one of its pews had been rented, for fifty dollars a year, by "A. Lincoln." Oral historians passed down the understanding that, upon coming to Washington, the divided nation's newly-elected leader had sought "a suitable church home … [led by] a clergyman who holds himself aloof from politics." President Lincoln was known to attend the mid-week prayer meetings, sitting on the far side of a glass-topped door left ajar. In the tragic days of those four years, his late nights were often spent walking along the south portico of the White House with his pastor. Inscribed in the Lincoln

Memorial, the 1864 Inaugural Address – touching on the question of divine providence and using Biblical allusions – echoed refrains from sermons heard from The New York Avenue Presbyterian Church's pulpit.

This was the tradition inherited and carried on by the Reverend Peter Marshall. He ministered to Presidents, Members of Congress, Justices of the United States Supreme Court. Long lines formed around his church each Sunday in anticipation of compelling sermons directed to this congregation and the Washington community at-large.

As Senate Chaplain from 1947 until his sudden death two years later, he opened its daily sessions with prayer and privately counseled its members: Not on politics or public policy, but on values, Scriptural lessons, and insights into life, public and private, which undoubtedly influenced their public service. Fame ensued; and his influence spread well beyond the District of Columbia.

Peter Marshall's lilting, wartime voice lifted the nation's spirits. Subsequently, as a new world order was crafted in Washington's corridors of power, his spiritual perspective was evident.

The last photograph of Dr. Marshall was taken at President Truman's inaugural on January 20, 1949; it shows the Senate Chaplain walking side-by-side with U.S. Senator Arthur Vandenberg – Chairman of the Senate Foreign Relations Committee. Formerly a New Deal adversary, diehard isolationist and long an opponent to American involvement in World War II, he had, by this time, surprisingly become a principal architect of a bipartisan foreign policy and supporter of the Marshall Plan, NATO, and the United Nations. This Republican President Pro Tempore of the Senate – among Members of Congress and other national leaders in The New York Avenue Presbyterian Church's congregation – had regularly sat in its pews. And they heard that "the airplane and the radio have annihilated time and distance … and the tragedy is that our vision, our faith, and our love have not expanded."

Humility, broadened perspectives, and reconciliation were reiterative threads of Dr. Marshall's sermons and Senate prayers. Seasoning these recurrent themes, his puckish charm and Scottish brogue undoubtedly contributed to the tempering of that period's ideological certainties.

Notwithstanding his personal relationships with political leaders and

The Rev. Dr. Peter Marshall, U.S. Senate Chaplain (far left) and Senator Arthur Vandenberg, president pro tempore, lead Senators onto the platform for the inauguration of Harry S. Truman on January 20, 1949.

increasing national attention, Peter Marshall's fundamental mission was ministry. His sermons' poignant lessons and the plain-spoken wisdom of his theology are, to me, what especially warrant continuing, contemporaneous reflection.

He believed that the preacher's fundamental role is to "persuade men and women to discover and to do the will of God in their everyday lives."

If we accept – or, at least, grasp – Luther's notion of "a priesthood of all believers," then these teachings have import not only for those wearing a clerical collar or aspiring to professional ministry. From these Lectures, Dr. Marshall's sermons and Senate prayers, and his widow's writings and memories, we can be certain that he believed that the work of ministering, encouraging and healing is not to be pursued only in churches or synagogues, or in Bible studies or mosques. He found, and saluted, works of grace in offices, schools and the marketplace, at homes, and on playgrounds.

> "You will find preachers among the poets /
> > And the playwrights. /
> > And occasionally a motion picture will preach a sermon and leave an impression in the mind and hearts of a movie audience that would be quite beyond most of us.

"Even "in picture houses," as he would say.

These Zimmerman Lectures were delivered on May 10-13, 1944 – at the eve of D-Day – only thirteen years after Dr. Marshall's own graduation and with no sense of how few years of his Christian ministry and life remained. Their message was directed to students preparing for Lutheran ordination. His words speak, however, as much to the saints and sinners among us as to those who are officially ordained to religious vocations.

He calls us all to be, in his Christian terms, "His ambassadors."

This was a master storyteller. Peter Marshall's sermons evoked the sights and sounds, smells, and even tastes of Biblical stories. His words – and his distinctive styles both of organization and oration – made the God of Scripture as tangible and real to his listeners as were their daily-lives' burdens and joys.

There is an undeniable alchemy in the use of powerful stories. They change us. His preaching – a vivid re-telling of deeply meaningful stories – resonated profoundly, influencing the lives and ministries of tens of scores of future "preachers." And his stories have touched innumerable lives, both in his lifetime and for generations thereafter.

His Zimmerman Lectures recognized, as might we all, that congregations and communities are

> "[M]en and women who … have been seared with sorrows /
> > Torn with temptation /

Discouraged by disappointments. /

Their feelings have been hurt /

Their hearts have been broken …

"By trouble they have either been made better or have become bitter."

He alerted the prospective ministers that their work would be "a merry-go-round of activity" and charged them to "constantly remember that the church is not an exhibition gallery for saints, but a school for sinners."

For him, the ideal minister is not necessarily from Hollywood's central casting. Effective ministry, he contended, can be achieved by a variety of personalities, skills, styles, and roles. The Zimmerman audience was introduced, for example, to Alabama's Brother Bryan, neither well-read nor an orator, "yet he had more influence in the city of Birmingham than any man who ever lived." Referencing Jesus' own ministry, Dr. Marshall posited that, "[h]ad we been a board of examiners to pass on candidates for discipleship, we would have turned down every one of the twelve": "They were ordinary men." Peter Marshall acknowledged his own mortal shortcomings.

> "[T]here is a discrepancy between what you preach and your own
>
> life .. and you will, if you are worth your salt, be troubled by this, as
> I am troubled by it in my own life."

Nevertheless, "[i]f we allow the Spirit of God to work through us, even our weaknesses may become our strength." Indeed, "you are a man," he underscored. …

Only men?

This was a man of the 1940s and 1950s. Virtually all Christian ministers were men. "Man" was the pronoun generally used to reference both genders. In that era, he, and millions of others, smoked cigarettes. Bowling leagues were hugely popular across socio-economic divides. Racial diversity, in his vernacular, was addressed as "Colored and white." He describes "the government of China" (then led by Chiang-Kai-shek) as "the most Christian government among the United Nations." But such anachronisms and what subsequent generations would consider "politically incorrect" terms should not distract us from Dr. Marshall's sermons' substance and spirit.

Theologically, he describes himself as "a theological conservative":

"The Bible is the most important book known to mankind. It has been the source of life and light for untold millions."

"His word, written by inspired men, will indict them as well as give them comfort and hope."

Yet there is a profound humility in Reverend Peter Marshall's proclamation of Truth.

In these Lectures, he admits that "some of it [*i.e.,* Scripture] is too deep for the wisest man," that he did not understand the Book of Revelation. He acknowledges contradictions in the Bible: "The fact that their [*i.e.,* "the authors of Scripture"] writings are gathered together in the canon does not mean that they thought the same way."

The sometimes-controversial opinions of a subsequent generation of theologians are presaged by his observations:

"Each of the books in the Bible was written in a particular historical background and for the purpose of meeting a definite historical situation." [So] "Before we can understand the author's message, we must ask what were the circumstances at the time of the writing ... and what were the circumstances of those to whom he wrote."

He cautions us as to "the delicacy and the danger in extracting the eternal principles from a particular piece of sacred writing."

"The Word of God does not exist in a vacuum but is set in the midst of life," he grants.

For this extraordinary, "ordinary" man whose life was committed to the vocation of Christian ministry, "The application of Scripture to our day lies in the eternal principles it contains, not in the literal situation that drew it forth."

Perhaps surprisingly, these Lectures note, even celebrate, a range of beliefs and doubts on a broad spectrum of doctrines and faith:

"Do not be deluded into thinking that the creek you know is all the ocean."

"You will find that, in life, there is always this 'nevertheless.'"

As if to predict that future of communities of faith will be called to navigate an increasingly secular American and European society, he remarks,

"It may well be that the Church is even now in the birth-throes of a new conception of the providence."

He seems to respond empathetically to those who struggle with conventional Christian doctrine. While summoning Americans to Christianity, he did not explicitly discourage those who may be moved to explore spirituality in dimensions far from his own experience and beliefs.

Yet the final lines of these Lectures – in his own handwriting – declaratively emphasize his foundational conviction: "There is only one Book to tell them."

Could this Presbyterian "man of the cloth" have declared his fundamental belief with greater conviction?

It may be observed, however, that not academic theology, but the practice of the presence of God and the life and teachings of Jesus were at Peter Marshall's core. Remember, he tells those seminary students and us, that

"[Christ] did not talk much about prayer – He prayed. /

He did not lecture on healing –He healed. … /

He did not argue about the sanctity of the temple – He strode in and cleaned it out personally."

Peter Marshall – an individual truly of, and engaged in, his own era – was a man of action as well as thought. He charged these seminary students to "[find] time" – as his Senate chaplaincy particularly demonstrated – "to keep ourselves abreast of current thinking" and worldly current events.

He lived in a period of Nazi and Fascist Europe. And his point that "So God today can use Hitler." undoubtedly raised eyebrows in that Zimmerman audience. But it continues to foster searching reflection on how the Creator acts in every age and in everyday life.

Threats, misguided leadership, sin, and seemingly apocalyptic challenges have plagued institutions, governments, and citizens throughout history. No wonder that his Lectures quote Paul: "We struggle not against flesh and blood, but against the ruling spirits of this dark age."

So much of these Lectures – noting divorce, abortions, and race riots, for example – apply to persistent issues of the human condition.

Dr. Marshall calls these students, and us, to be in this world, but not of this world. His challenge? Do not be fearful to proclaim eternal verities in the marketplace: "Have you ever known anybody, outside the pulpit, who was quiet and sober about truth?" Be courageous, he exhorts, in this "chivalrous adventure" of life and faith.

On the morning of December 7, 1941, Reverend Peter Marshall, addressing the U.S. Naval Academy's Class of '42 midshipmen at Annapolis, set aside his prepared remarks at the last minute and preached a prophetic message. Within an hour after he sat down, news of imperial Japan's attack at Pearl Harbor engulfed the nation. He had said, "I am one of those who believe that there are some principles worth fighting for and worth dying for, if need be."

"God permits war in order that we might see what sin really is."

He cautioned: "the trouble with our time is that, when we can't believe there is anything left to us worth dying for, then we're not sure there's anything worth living for either …."

Like a fruitful ministry or a faithful life, distance walking requires careful thought of what to take and what to leave behind. There are never enough maps or fellow travelers to consult, but you are ill-advised to rely entirely on them.

Some things you simply cannot control, and not just the weather. But as hikers like to say, "A man who was never lost never went very far."

Each person has a natural rhythm and routine.

There are no shortcuts.

Every long-distance hiker knows that you always need a destination but learns that you had better not feel defeated if one day's mark is missed. Your feet may be sore, your ankles swollen; but Lord willing, tomorrow's another day. You can take pride in having gone more than halfway, but there are still miles to go.

To some, the walk may seem straightforward and easy. Not so.

There are five points on a compass – North, South, East, West and where you are. And the last is most important, though often the most difficult to discern. That was the place where those students listening to the Zimmerman Lectures were seeking to find for themselves.

And that – where each of us is, spiritually – is likely the place we, too, are continuing to strive to discern.

Twelve months in walking boots, as well as in pinstripes, taught me the truth of the Spanish proverb, "There are no roads. Roads are made by walking."

Though the road may be uncertain, we can, I believe, find guidance, exhilaration, and comfort walking in the company of Peter Marshall.

Godspeed

Philip Lader
United States Ambassador to the
Court of St. James's
(1997-2001)

A NOTE TO READERS

In *A Man Called Peter*, Catherine Marshall's biography adapted into the film by the same name, she reveals what made her husband's preaching so extraordinary.

Dr. Marshall's congregation always marveled at his reading of the Scriptures. He could take the most difficult Pauline passage and read it with such understanding and lucidity that it sprang into life. What few people knew was that he had mastered the art of reading aloud, when, as a boy, sitting before the fire in the long winter evenings, he had read the Bible hours at a time to his blind grandmother.

Dr. Marshall's art in the pulpit was an unlearned art. All the tricks of great oratory, as well as the actor's skill, he employed unconsciously. He had the poet's feeling for descriptive words. Occasionally he would let himself go on the description of a sunset or the hills of Scotland. From these oratorical ventures he acquired the nickname of Twittering-birds Marshall from the four fellow ministers with whom he lunched on Fridays. One of these ministers once remarked wryly, "He has the language to gild the lily and pin ruffles on the stars."

His diction was almost perfect. A university speech professor advised his students to listen to either Orson Welles or Peter Marshall, if they wanted to hear perfect diction.

Like all great preachers down through the ages, Dr. Marshall said nothing new, but he said it in a new way. The huge congregations which regularly packed the church and over-flowed into downstairs rooms were gripped anew by the gospel.

Catherine Marshall

THE ZIMMERMAN LECTURES ON EFFECTIVE PREACHING

The Lectures in Effective Preaching were established in memory of Jeremiah Zimmerman (1848-1930), an 1873 graduate of Pennsylvania (later Gettysburg) College, of which he was a trustee from 1917 until his death.

Zimmerman served most of his life as an ordained pastor in Syracuse, New York, after traveling extensively in his early years, visiting the tombs of patriarchs, and embarking on a twenty-eight month trip around the world, which led to his becoming a numismatic authority.

The Lecture series was inaugurated on April 17-20, 1928, by Dr. James I. Vance of Nashville. Dr. Peter Marshall was preceded by noted speakers such as George A. Buttrick and James Moffat; he was succeeded in May 1945 by preeminent theologian Reinhold Niebuhr (1892-1971) drawing the five lectures from his 1932 book, *Moral Man and Immoral Society: A Study in Ethics and Politics.*

THE ZIMMERMAN LECTURES ON EFFECTIVE PREACHING

Delivered by
The Reverend Dr. Peter Marshall
Gettysburg Seminary
May 10–13, 1944

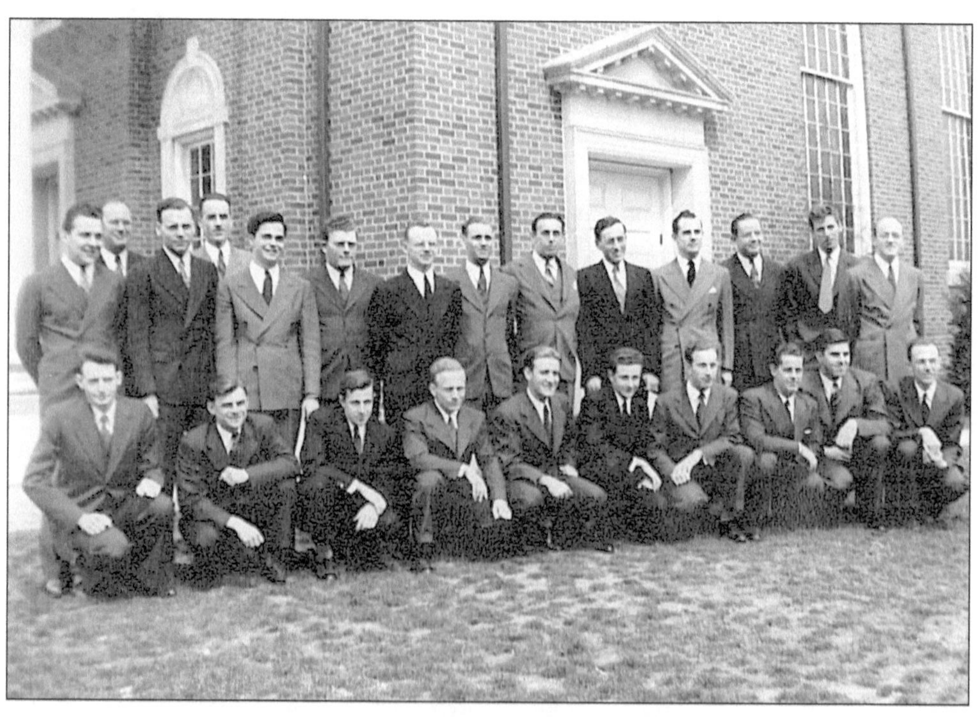

The Class of 1944, now Lutheran Theological Seminary

Selected Shorts on Preaching

I count it an honor and a privilege to be with you this week, and to be invited to deliver the Zimmerman Lectures on Effective Preaching.

I sincerely believe that all that <u>could</u> be said about preaching
has already been said, and said most eloquently by such men
as Phillips Brooks, Frank Cairns, James Black, William
Adams Brown, George A. Buttrick, Ralph Sockman and
their company, who in lectures here, at Yale, and in other
seminaries in this country and abroad, have covered the field.

So I have thought it well to confine myself to some practical aspects
of our common task. I have sought to view effective preaching from the
perspective of my own study and pulpit and congregation.

Therefore I have, quite arbitrarily, divided the lectures
into five sections, namely:

   "The Man"
      "The Message"
         "The Vision"
            "The Method"
               "The Setting."

Or, if you prefer a less stilted series of topics, I might offer:

   "The Producer"
      "The Script"
         "Lights! "
            "Camera! "
               "Action!"[1]

To assist in oral delivery, Peter Marshall adapted to his own needs a format he first learned from Dr. Trevor Mordecai of Birmingham, Alabama, a Welshman whose preaching he had much admired. The Editors have retained his distinctive format in presenting these Lectures.

Peter Marshall in the Pulpit
The New York Avenue Presbyterian Church in Washington, D.C.

I

THE PRODUCER

The Man

God has chosen us for His ambassadors ....

> Christ has no hands but our hands
>> To do his work today;
> He has no feet but our feet
>> To lead men in his way;
> He has no tongue but our tongues
>> To tell men how he died;
> He has no help but our help
>> To bring them to his side.[2]

In one sense God has to take us just as we are.

It is His glory that he can make us more than we are.

If we allow the Spirit of God to work through us,

even our weaknesses may become our strength.

The preacher perhaps more than any other person

will discover the stark reality of Christ's

statement

> "Without me ye can do nothing."[3]

But if he will dedicate all that he is and all

that he has to the service of Him who whispered

him in the ear, he may even shout with Paul,

> "I can do all things through Christ
> Which strengtheneth me."[4]

When you consider the twelve men whom Jesus chose
as his disciples, you must agree that had we been
members of an investigating committee

or a board of examiners to pass on candidates
for discipleship, we would have turned down every
one of the twelve.
Why did Jesus select the men He did?
Well Mark gives us a clue, for in his gospel we
read that he selected twelve in order "that they
might be with Him."[5]
They were ordinary man, and yet after Pentecost
they were so powerfully used that they were
described by their enemies as "these that have
turned the word upside down."[6]
If Christ, through the Holy Spirit could do that to
the loud-mouthed sons of Thunder . . .

to the blustering, impulsive Peter
to the dogmatic unbelieving Thomas . . .
What can He do to you and me if we will give Him
the opportunity?
We are dedicated to serve Christ in and through the
church, and we must constantly remember that the church
is not an exhibition gallery for saints, but a school
for sinners.[7]
It is not a memorial organization—organized for the
purpose of keeping fresh a pious legend

or a sacred memory . . . .
It is a fellowship of believers "apprehended by God
in Christ who associate together in the spirit of
common humility and service."[8]

We are not going out —you and I—"on our own."
Our ordination vows will tie us very close to our
comrades in our battalion, it is true, but we are to
march with other battalions in the regiment
of Christ which is His church.
To each of us going forward under the banner of the
Cross there comes the challenge to maintain the honor
of the regiment.
And yet we are not in a parade.
The ministers of religion are not drum-majors strutting
blandly ahead of blaring churches through streets
lined with social misfits

                moral cripples

                        industrial wrecks

                                and victims of war.

No, it is not a parade, gentlemen, that takes us
through the streets …
It is rather a campaign in a war that knows no armistice[9]
and that finds us most of the time under fire in a
sort of "no-man's- land."
Our position is made the more difficult because all of
our witness, our work and our worries will fall under three
heads, namely, those of the person

                the pastor

                      and the preacher.

As a person, you are a man, equipped and endowed
with all the appetites

                longings

                    desires

                          and passions with which

other men have to deal—you are like them.
All the temptations that leer at them through the
casement windows of their hearts leer at you.
All the siren voices that entice them will drift
 your way also ….
and many more, that other men never hear.
 "I am a Jew!" cried Shylock in the *Merchant of Venice*[10]
 "Hath not a Jew eyes?
 Hath not a Jew hands, organs, dimensions,
 senses, affections, passions?
Fed with the same food,
 hurt with the same weapons,
 subject to the same diseases,
healed by the same means,
 warmed and cooled by the same winter and summer
as a Christian is?
If you prick us, do we not bleed?
If you tickle us, do we not laugh?
 If you poison us, do we not die?
And if you wrong us, shall we not revenge?
If we are like you in the rest, we will resemble
you in that."
You will often have reason to mediate upon Shylock's
outburst, and to wish that your people would
remember that the man in the pulpit is a man.
But he is more than that … he is a pastor
 a shepherd of souls ….
feeling a responsibility for each one committed
to his care ….
and feeling his keenest anguish when some of the

sheep over whom he has been appointed under-shepherd

refuse to accept his ministrations.

He is also a preacher required "to deliver a religious

message at regular intervals regardless of his own feeling"[11]

> the state of his health
> the demands of his time
> his own personal problems
> the weather

or any other of the many circumstances that regulate

the size of his congregation or the extent of their

interest.

I sometimes agree with Heywood Broun who said:

"Perhaps the pulpit might regain the public

respect if the minister who realized that

he has no message on a given Sunday were to

rise and frankly announce 'Maybe next week,

but not today.'"

After all,

> "We are the music-makers,
>> We are the dreamers of dreams,
> Wandering by lone sea-breakers,
>> And sitting by desolate streams;
> World-losers and world-forsakers,
>> On whom the pale moon gleams;
> We are the movers and shakers
>> Of the world forever, it seems.[12]

You who graduate this week have been trained for the ministry …

and yet you must realize that your seminary cannot do

it all.

There are so many things that no professor can give

you … so many things you did not find in your text-
books.
And with regard to what your professors and text-books
have given you, it may be years before it becomes
apparent to you.
Even now, thirteen years after my own graduation,[13] I am
Just beginning to grasp some of the things that the
professor hammered home for three years.
Perhaps they were hammered so far into my head that
only now, are they working up into the conscious.
You have been trained for the ministry, and this week
you say farewell at your port of embarkation.
So what?
We as persons are pastors
          and preachers
and our three functions must work in unity and
cooperation, because preaching in the definition
of Phillips Brooks is "the communication of truth
     by man to men, which has in it two essential
     elements, truth and personality, neither of
     those can be sacred and still be preaching.[14]
I shall not here raise the question of your call,
for that is a matter too personal
     too delicate and sacred for the
cross examination of any third party.
But this I will say, the man who has not truly been
called to preach and who is not constantly tapping
the line of divine power and strength and guidance,
will be one of those preachers described by Ralph
Sockman as,

"matches, in that they carry all their
brilliance in their own hands, and the first
flare soon fades. They lack that sustained
incandescence which comes from a current of
power surging through them from a greater
source."[15]

"Preaching is not the art of making and delivering
sermons. It is more than that.
Preaching, according to Bishop William A. Quayle,
Is "the art of making a preacher and delivering
That ... the sermon is the preacher up to date."[16]
"The minister of religion is committed to the cure
of souls and as such he is a doctor of humanity."
Let me assure you that "it is more difficult to
become a doctor of humanity than it is to become
a doctor of divinity."[17]
Ralph Sockman says that "for the former, one must
cultivate all classes and conditions of men
while for the latter he need cultivate only one
college president."
The Discipline
We must guard ourselves against the error of giving
the centre of the stage to the unimportant.
It is true that many causes will clamour for our
support, but we dare not emulate the earnest but
uncoordinated enthusiast who "mounted his horse and
rode off in all directions."[18]
Nothing should crowd out your own quiet time in the
morning.

And it is here that I feel most ashamed and like a hypocrite.
But this I do know, and say to you with all the
conviction at my command, that those days when we have
talked with God, and meditated upon His will for our lives …
      and sought His guidance,
will be days of accomplishment and victory, as
compared with the other days of futility and
frustration and wrestling without avail.[19]
I have found it virtually impossible to adhere to any
rigid schedule ….
Yet our time must be allocated with economy and purpose.
The preacher's work is not the doing of certain
      specific duties.
You cannot set down on paper, just what you are going
to do …
      and when …
            and for how long.
Too many things arise to throw your schedule off your
desk and into your wastebasket.
I have no right to tell you that you ought to take a
day off—or at least some time each week for
exercise and recreation ….
For I myself take no day off …
      and get very little exercise and recreation …
although during the bowling season I have spent one
evening each week bowling in a church league.
This is a case, however, when I claim the right to
 be pleased that you will do as I say …
      and not as I do.

[Henry C.] Link in *The Return to Religion* says that man could
force himself to do some things which he does
not desire ... for 'he believes that by doing
what he dislikes, [a man] is administering a
wholesome discipline to his own soul."[20]
There was a time when I said, with regard to
certain matters very distasteful to me:

 "nobody will ever get me to do them,

   That's one thing, I'll never do."
I have to confess to you, rather gratefully, that
I have done every one of them.
"Humility is a virtue all preach, never practice;

 and yet everybody is content to hear."[21]
There are times when the minister is called upon
to apologize and to make the first overtures in
some misunderstanding ....
When he knows beyond a peradventure of a doubt,
that he is in the right.
It is because he knows he is in the right, that
he can assume the blame.
I suppose you are familiar with the modern epitaph:

 "This is the grave of Mike O'Day,

   who died maintaining his right of way.

 His right was clear, his will was strong,

   but he's just as dead as if he'd been wrong."[22]
This discipline is not forced upon the minister.
It is given to him, and he accepts it with the
eyes of Christ upon him, for is he not a pastor and
a servant of all?

A pastor can't lose his people—as long as they can

be won—and what is the minister's price, who is

a servant of Him Who "humbled Himself and made

Himself of no reputation?"

So far in this lecture, I have spoken of the

numerous details which thrust themselves necessarily

upon us as ministers.

They cannot be escaped. They must be met … and

mastered.

He has a responsibility to his wife and children,

for not only is he a minister

a pastor

and a preacher …

he is also a breadwinner …

and the Lord requires of him that he shall be a good

provider.

As the young minister works with individuals, he soon

finds that these individuals are as much influenced by

his own private life

   his actions

  and his experiences in the Christian life

as they are by what he says in the pulpit.

However trite it is, it is still trust that we must

"practice what we preach" and

"actions speak louder than words."

For the man in the street is quick to note any

hypocrisy, and is not at all reluctant to comment upon it.

If a choice were necessary, a minister's life would count

far more for the kingdom of God if he were a great

man but a poor preacher, than if he were a great preacher
but a poor Christian.

One of the most influential preachers I have ever known
or heard of was Brother Bryan of Birmingham, Alabama.[23]
He was no orator
    His sermons were homiletically poor
        He read very little outside of the Bible …
and yet he had more influence in the city of
Birmingham than any man who ever lived.
It was his life and his character.
    It was what he did much more than what he said.
It was his love for people—colored and white
        Greeks
      Italians
    Jews and Gentiles
that won him the love of the whole community.
Firemen and policemen
    prostitutes and pickpockets
        bums and bankers came to pay tribute when the
city's pastor died.
Let us never forget that Christ Himself probably
preached a few sermons.
He did not talk much about prayer—He prayed.
He did not lecture on healing—He healed …
He did not argue about the sanctity of the temple—
    He strode in and cleaned it out personally.[24]
He wrote no book on immortality … He simply
rose from the dead.

In saying this, I am not, of course, offering any

brief on behalf of poor preaching ….

I am praying with Paul that we may be given a message

and that that message will be the spontaneous

overflow of a rich and abundant Christian life.

You will be aware very soon that there is a

discrepancy between what you preach and your own

life … and you will, if you are worth your salt,

be troubled by this, as I am troubled by it in my

own life.

You will find yourself face to face with a dilemma.

You must proclaim your loftiest ideals—the best

you know—from the pulpit ….

and yet you will find yourself unable to live up

to that highest ideal in your own life.

I preach that prayer changes things ….

    and that a daily prayer habit is essential

to the nurture of the Christian life ….

And yet, even as I say this, I am keenly aware of

the inadequacy of my own prayer life.

When I am most true to the New Testament, I uphold

absolute purity not only of body but of mind … and motive …

and yet, at times I am keenly aware that I have

compromised with evil in my thinking and in my

acting.

I preach forgiveness and point out that our forgiveness by God depends
upon our willingness to forgive others ….

and yet I find it hard to forgive certain church officers who block certain
programs in the church's activity ….

I find it hard to bear and forbear with those men and women

who, like the slowest ship in the convoy, make the

fast ships slow down to their speed.

We must preach absolute dependence upon God …

and yet we will wonder may times if it is not our

salary checks upon which we are depending.

You will soon[25] become aware of these discrepancies in your ministry.

But there is something even more important than that, and that is

whether the discrepancy becomes wider or narrower as the years go

by.

There are some words I cannot read without a blush.

    "or how wilt thou say to thy brother, Let me

    Pull out the mote out of thine eye; and behold

    A beam is in thine own eye. Thou hypocrite."[26]

As a pastor you must always remember that you have

certain denominational responsibilities.

You are a member of a presbytery and a synod,

and implicit in your ordination vows is the obligation

to work with your fellow ministers.

The lone eagle not only is condemned to a loneliness

of the heart and spirit, but to the loss of that sense

of fellowship which is so vital to every minister.

In our vows we undertake to "study the peace, the purity, and the unity

of the Church,"[27]

And it is the tragedy and the shame of Protestantism

that this vow is broken again and again.

The controversies that arise within the church bring

the Gospel into disrepute because they reveal such an

absence of the Spirit of Christ.

In a newspaper report of a religious group[28] meeting in

New York City, this comment was made:

"When they come to deal with the disagreement

on an article of doctrine, they are filled with

bitterness and eaten with hate. Not one note

of humility of Jesus is found in the

speech of these men ....

not one note of charity

not one not of forgiveness

not one note of gentleness.

But instead curses and pugnacity,

Fire and brimestone

And all uncharitableness"[29]

I myself am a theological conservative.

I believe in the virgin birth

inspiration of scripture

the substitutionary atonement

the bodily resurrection

and the second coming ...

and yet I must confess how difficult it is for me

to have fellowship with some of my brethren who in

their defense of one or another of these doctrines

fail to reveal the spirit of Christ. They become

so bitter ... so dogmatic ...

they say such mean things about their brethren

that I cannot believe that the nail-scarred hands

of Christ are lifted over them in blessing.

As pastors we will have to deal with people in

the church who do not like us personally and whom.

we may not personally like.

I fully subscribed to the statement which I believe

was attributed to Hugh Black.

    "I love everybody but there are

    some people I don't like."[30]

At times, when we as men of conviction, may be tempted

to say to some who are manifestly out of harmony

with the church's program, "O, go to the Devil" …

Since he is obviously using them …

we must refrain lest they become completely his.

As pastors we must continue to woo and hope and

pray eventually to win.

We are administrators of a church program …

and that involves women's groups and men's groups …

mission work

    And young people's activities

    The Church Bible School

        The official boards ….

It involves budgets and finances

    baptisms

        weddings

    and funerals ….

It involves pastoral calls

        and personal counseling

    preparing programs and arranging services …

a merry-go-round of activity, in which, like the music

we "go round and round" although the place where we

come out is not always clear.

As the preacher, you are definitely "on the spot," because

with all these demands on your time, you have still

only twenty-four hours in the day …

    and seven days in the week.

No matter how much of your time has been consumed in

the routine administration of your parish …

no matter how many calls have been made upon you by

    people in need …

no matter how many conferences were demanded …

no matter how many emergencies arose ….

You still are under the tyranny of the calendar and the clock.

When eleven o'clock comes on Sunday morning, you must

go into the pulpit with a message …

and your people expect it of you, because the great

part of your congregation has no idea of all the

demands that are made …

And those who do know of the demands still expect

that somehow—because you are a preacher—you

will have something to say.

What you have to preach is the word of God …

    the eternal truth ….

You have to bring a message to needy souls ….

You are not at liberty to preach what you please, you

Must preach what you see the people need.

There are times when you will feel empty—like the

chest of drawers in which Mr. Boy Sawyer showed to Mr. Winkle in his
little surgery:

    "Dammies, my dear boy," said he to his impressed

    Astonished visitor:

    "half the drawers have nothing in them

    And the other half don't open."[31]

Nevertheless, because the clock says it is time to

preach—preach you must.

Our problem is to come up with a message despite

the distractions

    the intrusions

        and the interruptions of the week before.

Michelangelo, it is said, "used to carry a candle stuck on his forehead in a pasteboard cup which kept his own shadow from being cast upon his work while he with skillful chisel carved his incomparable statues."[32]

As we stand in the pulpit, our people must see—

not us —but Christ.

One of our difficulties is finding time to keep

ourselves abreast of current thinking …

in the last religious books.

    current events

    social issues and trends.

Today we have become specialists in nearly everything.

School teachers have their specialized fields

where formerly the teacher taught mathematics

        and history

      and geography

    and science

    and perhaps a language or two ….

Now he has his own field—one or two subjects …

he is a specialist.

So, too, in medicine

the general practitioner is fast disappearing.

our doctors have become so highly specialized that

the patient is sometimes bewildered.

Yet, the preacher, to minister to all the specialists
in his congregation, must be informed in many fields—
have a broad acquaintance and interest in the narrow
interest of his people ….
For he has to apply Christian principles to every
field of human thought and action.
The preacher can capture the interests of his
hearer in the preacher's message, by an intelligent
reference to a particular field of the hearer's
interest ….
but he must have care that his reference is accurate -
else he forfeits his hearer's respect.
Having delivered his sermon, the preacher must hear in
the echoes of his own mind and hear the cry
"Excelsior."[33]

As prophets we must denounce evils, even although we are not always
or often able to indicate the solution to the problems.

We have to stand for something—the principles which
Christ taught and we have to set them down in our
modern world …
in the midst of the situations that cry out for remedy.
I need not enlarge upon the problems that confront
America today, for every thoughtful Christian is
acutely aware of them:
One marriage in every five[34] in America ends in divorce.
There are now half a million abortions annually …
Race riots in Boston, Detroit and Los Angeles are
ominous portends of things to come ….[35]
In the District of Columbia the per capita consumption
of hard liquor now amounts to about four and a half

gallons per year ….

In America there are more laws and more lawlessness

than in any other country in the world.[36]

We need to recapture the passion of the prophets,

for the prophet always laid his emphasis on life,

    on conduct

     and on moral quality.

"The prophet irritates

     he prods

    he denounces

  he stands alone in his demands,

Insists on applying God's eternal principles of life.

He is a dangerous disturber of men's minds.

He constantly strikes at immorality

    at vice

  and organized evil." [37]

whether in high places or in low.

We think of Jesus as the "Prince of Peace" … which He was;

  as "Gentle Jesus, meek and mild" … which He was;

but we forget that He was also one of the

angriest men who ever lived.

All the saints and prophets were angry men—

grousing in public places

  nailing denunciations on cathedral doors.

They were angry about specific things and

specific people whose names were household names.

How superbly Paul expressed it: "We struggle not

against flesh and blood, but against the ruling

spirits of this dark age."[38]

There is need for us to know that we are in a conflict.
There have always been some great souls who took
The Gospel terribly to heart—Paul

    Augustine—Francis of Assisi
Latimer and Ridley[39]

    Martin Luther

        Calvin and John Knox ….
David Livingstone[40]

      Carey

       Adoniram Judson[41]

      William Grenfell

     Father Damien of Molokai

    Albert Schweitzer

    Jane Addams

   Kegawa
Bishop Bergraff[42]

   and Martin Niemueller.[43]
Gentlemen, our calling has its dangers—for it is
a chivalrous adventure.
I could not enumerate all the dangers you are
likely to face, for you go different places
and you will by God's grace carry out your commissions
in different ways ….

But each man will wrestle with the beasts in his own Ephesus.
But make no mistake about it—the beasts are
still there!
It is a law of mechanics, that work put in equals
work got out.

The battery in your car is capable of supplying

current to your spark plugs

    sounding your horn

and giving you light when darkness comes …

but it has to be recharged itself … as you run.

The car carries a generator with it … so that current

is being made even as it is being expended.

Apply that procedure to your ministry … else you will

find sooner than you think … that your battery has

run down.

You must have a spiritual generator …

a sermonic intake to cope with the drain that will be

made upon you.

    "And this our life, exempt from public haunt,

        finds tongues in trees, books in the running brooks

        sermons ins stones, and good in everything."[44]

Beware of riding your hobbies in the pulpit.

The saddle sores that come will pain your people as

well as you.

Richard Baxter "preached as never sure to preach again,

    And as a dying man to dying men."[45]

Yes, but it can be done—and should be done—in different ways.

Do not be deluded into thinking that the creek you know

is all the ocean.

I once preached four sermons in a western city, and

when later I was considered by the pulpit committee,

a majority of the congregation voted not to extend me

the call …

one of their reasons being that I had preached four sermons

and had not once mentioned the second coming of our Lord.[46]
In determining the balance and proportion of your
preaching,
Scriptural proportion is a good guide.
Every ministry that is sympathetic will reveal pests—
male and female—mostly the latter,
who will not only weary you with their problems—real and
imaginary …
but sorely try your patience and your Christian grace. [47]
You are caught in a dilemma.
If you are short and abrupt with them, they can accuse
you of being unsympathetic and refusing to help.
If you are courteous, they will be encouraged and
make life miserable for you in many feminine ways.
The minister seems to have an attraction for certain
types of women and no danger is more real than
this one.
In your zeal for your parish work, and your
willingness to be of service to all who need you,
do not neglect your own family.
They need you too.
They love you and you owe something to them.
Remember, when you marry, you are a husband and
a father, as well as a pastor.
I shall not soon forget the indictment I heard in
our little boy's prayer one night, when he thanked
the Lord that He let his daddy stay home that evening.[48]
Another danger of the clergyman's life is self-
indulgence.

Just because you don't have to punch a time clock

And are not made to account for every day's

activities, do not surrender to your moods and feel

that the church owes you a living whether you work

or not.

Laziness—physical as well as intellectual—is so

real a danger that no minister can speak of it without blushing.

Would you confess that you are conceited?

Most of us are—when we leave seminary.

Perhaps we were sought after by the seminary, if

we are in a church that has more than one school

of the prophets.

It makes us feel important, and that somehow,

we are conferring an honor upon the seminary by

consenting to attend it rather than its rival.

Phillips Brooks said: "A man's first wonder when

he begins to preach is that people do not come to

hear him. After a while, if he is good for anything,

 he begins to wonder what they do."[49]

In any real man, success will bring with it, humility.

You will find—and it is a joy to discover it—

an eager welcome awaiting you from your first

congregation ....

but it must not be hoped that the world generally

will greet you with that same enthusiasm ....

The people outside the Church—and they are now a

majority of our population—say with Don Juan,

"Let us have wine and women, mirth and laughter,

Sermons and soda water the day after."[50]

Your voice will be, in some respects, a disturbing
voice, in that it will plead for a consideration of
Christ and all He stands for in the world of today.
"Other movements may try to advance beyond their
founders, but Christianity's slogan of advance has
always been 'Back to Christ.'" …[51]
because what He said, probably in Aramaic in a little
land at the eastern end of the Mediterranean basin
nineteen hundred years ago, is still authoritative
for our times, just as if it had been said in English.
last night on the radio.
Therefore, we go to our tasks as Christian blacksmiths
with the hammer of the Word of God beating out on the
anvil of human need and desperation, a great theology.
Or in another figure of speech, we are to focus the magnifying
glass of God's Word upon the problems of our people
so that the Light of God's truth concentrated upon them
will burn until it bursts into the flame of complete
consecration.
Let no man deceive you: Your task has its own peculiar difficulties.
In your private life, you will soon discover that you
live like a goldfish in a bowl, and your every movement
is under constant scrutiny.
The spotlight of public office and leadership plays
upon you wherever you go and whatever you do, for you
are an example not only to your church, but to your
community as well.
The minister's family is exposed to the same
tribulations as any family in the congregation ….

And yet it must always rise above them … in

Christian grace and victory.

You will be plagued by leaking faucets

        and perhaps a leaking roof ….

You will have maid problems and difficulties …

and you and your wife do not always agree …

    and because you are human, you will be tempted to

be more like a man than a preacher.[52]

At times when you are tired and would like nothing

more than to put on your slippers and stretch in

an easy chair, you will have to go somewhere and

do something … putting your personal wishes aside.

You wear a uniform, and because you are a marked

man … whether by a clerical collar or by the

more subtle obligations of your office, …

you will be required to adhere to certain standards

of conduct.

The place you occupy will determine not only the

rightness or wrongness of an action …

but its propriety or impropriety.

No Christian minister would ever want to become addicted to alcohol

    or to become a gambler.

He would not indulge in "playing the daily double." …

And yet there are other parts of a community's

mores which are to be avoided because of the

subtle obligations of his position

A minister may not see any great moral harm in

Sunday ball games

or in a game of bridge

or in dancing with his young people in a

properly chaperoned well-conducted dance

attended by Christian young people ....[53]

he may enjoy the theater ...

And yet, there are times when out of consideration

for his influence and leadership he must deprive

himself of some things in which he does not see

any particular harm.

For through these details your witness be made real.

Sometimes to a man in the active ministry these details

seem to be clutching hands holding him back ....

He must lean against them as against a contrary wind.

but here is the heart of the matter:

Neville Chamberlain, in one of his first speeches as new

Prime Minister, likened the European situation to

mountainous snow banks of hatred so poised that a voice

might release and start an avalanche.[54]

We all know to our sorrow that there was a voice that

started the avalanche—the voice of Hitler.[55]

If such is the power of the voice that speaks evil,

the God who gives us the power to overcome evil, demands

that we speak His Word in no uncertain voice.

With fear and trembling, knowing our own unworthiness,

our ignorance

       intolerance

  our prejudice and our sin,

Nevertheless let us speak boldly the Word that must be spoken

the Truth that must endure ... for:

    "Who has known heights and depths, shall not again,

> know peace, not as the calm heart knows
> low ivied walls, a garden close
> the old enchantment of a rose.
> And though he <u>tread</u> the humble ways of men,
> he shall not speak the common tongue again.
> Who has known heights shall bear forevermore
> an incommunicable thing
> that hurts his heart, as if a wing
> beat at the portal, challenging:
> and yet, lured by the gleam his vision wore,
> who once has trodden stars seeks peace no more."
>
> —Mary Brent Whiteside[56]

This is the ultimatum of God's truth.

It is the call that is upon you.

As James Black says:[57]

"If there is anything that creates a peculiar
passion, it is truth.

It generates its own white heat.

And if you preach what you believe, as if you
believed it, as if it meant everything to you,
there will be a natural ring and passion in your
word that is infinitely better than any extraneous
type of eloquence.

In this connection, I have heard it said that the
truth should be quietly and soberly delivered,
and should be allowed to do its own gracious work.

But have you ever known anybody, outside the pulpit,
who was quiet and sober about truth?

"Truth is the one thing in every age and station

that has set the heather on fire.

It has led martyrs to the stake with shining eyes,

and turned the world upside down.

I can't understand a man, speaking of a topic

that concerns his own soul and the salvation of

man, preaching with casualness or insipidity.

"If only he is in earnest and speaks as if he believes,

there will be a ring even in his voice that will

command and arrest.

"Please do not be ashamed of the enthusiasm that

truth generates.

All the great ages of history have been ages of

enthusiasm, drunk with dreams.

It was sheer enthusiasm that built and held the

early Church, the passion of high belief, truth

held so dear that as compared with it life was cheap."[58]

That truth, gentlemen, has not changed!

Dr. Peter Marshall Engaged in Sermon Preparation
The New York Avenue Presbyterian Church Office

II.

____

THE SCRIPT

The Message

Our primary function is to preach.

It was for that God whispered us in the ear.

It was for that purpose God tapped us on the shoulder.[59]

We are under the compulsion of a call.

Preaching is our divine vocation.

Let us always remember that our work is a vocation—

not a job.

Amos was called from tending sheep

Elisha from the plow

Peter … Andrew … James … and John from their

fishing nets—to learn how to catch men …

Matthew in his customs office saw the beckoning

finger, closed the ledger and walked away ….

Dwight L. Moody went out from the shoe store ….

David Livingstone from the weaving mill

and Albert Schweitzer from the university ….

Whenever and however the call comes to a man he

must obey.

He who has been whispered in the ear must respond.

It is an imperious summons, and he will know no peace

until he gives himself to it.

There will be no peace or satisfaction in anything

else he tries to do.

If God has drafted him for the ministry, a man will

be miserable until he is inducted.

It is the highest calling on earth.

And while it behooves us "to think no more highly

of ourselves than we ought to think,"[60]

It is also true that we should let no man despise

our calling ....

And take care that we do not despise it ourselves.

As the stars make no apology for invading the midnight sky ....

As the tide sweeps hungrily without explanation

into every bay and inlet ....

As Christian ministers, it is our business to understand

the religion that we profess ....

and to be able to impart our knowledge to those who do not

possess it.

It matters little what else we know, if we do not know this,

for the mastery of no other theme can serve as a substitute

for ignorance here.

We must make men see God.

Our preaching must draw people to the kingdom of God, and

make them want to turn their lives over to <u>God</u> and His

control.

As they catch the vision of Christian service, they will

usually want to join the church.

Let us recognize at the outset that the Christian religion

is first and foremost a message about God.

It is not primarily a new ethic ....

It is not just a philosophy of brotherliness and loving
our neighbor …
and accepting the Golden Rule.
It is not a way of thinking or of looking at life.
Nor is it a social program. It includes all of these, to
be sure, but basically it is a message about God.
That message is this: that the living God—infinite
                                        eternal
                        and unchangeable
has at one definite point broken into history in an
unprecedented way.
Once and for all, in an actual life lived out upon this
earth, God has spoken, and has given a full and final
revelation of Himself. In Jesus, God has come!
Such is the dramatic and astounding statement on which
the Christian religion is built. That is the foundation
of it.
Yet Christianity is not merely fact. It is good news.
It came into the world as a message of redemption to
men in need.
It professed to bring forgiveness for sin
                                comfort in sorrow …
    guidance in perplexity
            strength in weakness
spiritual power for right living
and the promise of a better social order for mankind.
Its founder was the promised one
            the Messiah
    God incarnate in human flesh.

He had come to establish the Kingdom of God, and
to be the agent of His saving work.
It was impossible nineteen hundred years ago for men
to be indifferent to His claims.
He had to be accepted or rejected.
What He claimed was either true or false.
One must be for Christ or against Him.
And the first preachers of the Christian Church were
witnesses to the facts of the Christian religion—
namely, that Christ was the Messiah

                     the Promised One

            the Redeemer

      the Lamb of God which taketh away the sin

   of the world …
that He died on the cross for the remission of sin …
that He rose again from the dead, leaving the tomb empty …
that he ascended into Heaven and sitteth on the right

   hand of God the Father …
that he sent His Holy Spirit to change the lives of

   these very witnesses and all who would believe

   their message and trust Him Whom they preached.
The same power that had raised Christ from a physical
death had literally made them new creatures—with
new habits

   new desires

      and new personalities.
As we turn the pages of the New Testament, we find
there the dreamy platitude of the worldly wise—
"You can't change human nature" exultantly refuted
again and again.

The refrain of the first Christians was rather,

"we know it can be done, because it happened to us."

They had felt the fresh strong winds of the spirit

rushing through their lives, sweeping away the cobwebs

of prejudice

    superstition

          and meaningless religious practices.

No wonder they wanted to shout their message from the

house-tops …

no wonder it was like a fire in their bones until they

made it known.

Our message is first of all a message of personal

salvation ….

It speaks to the deep need of the human heart—

The need of forgiveness

the need of guidance

    the need of comfort

    the need of strength

  the need of inward harmony and peace.

Christianity—you see—is more than fact. It is a

message of good news, proclaiming salvation and

summoning to service.

Our preaching, then, must inspire and instruct those

who have already taken the first step—namely,

surrendering their hearts and wills to God's control.

It is at this point that one hears considerable

criticism of the average Protestant preaching.

People have said, "It is all very well to tell us what

we ought to do … but you do not tell us how to do it."

I think the point is well taken.
If, after his careful diagnosis, based upon his study and
his experience, the doctor were to place in the hands
of his patient a bottle of medicine or a box of pills,
and say,
    "Here is the remedy for your sickness. Take
      this and it will make you well."
He would fail in bringing the patient to the healing
he seeks.
He must also provide the patient with "instructions for
taking."
Is the medicine in the bottle to be used internally
or externally?
How much is to be taken in a single dose?
Should it be taken before meals or after?
Dangerous consequences might result from the doctor's
failure to instruct the patient how to take his
medicine.[61]
In the same way the preacher fails when he neglects
to instruct in the techniques of Christian living.
For example, we exhort our people to study the Bible,
but far too often we do not tell them how.
We advocate prayer—but we do not describe the
methods, and in far too many cases we fail to teach
its principles
    its rules
        and its requirements.
We speak of the availability of God's guidance in
our daily lives, and yet we leave to various sects

and groups the teaching of methods which may or may
not be valid, and which may even be dangerous.
Remember always that you are preaching to human
beings—men and women who have come to grips with
problems in their lives.
They have been seared with sorrows
            torn with temptations
discouraged by disappointments
their feelings have been hurt
      their hearts have been broken …
by trouble they have either been made better or have
become bitter.
You will see many a brave yet wan smile that hides
an aching heart.
You must root your preaching in reality, remembering
that these persons before you have problems
                    doubts
            fears
          and anxieties
gnawing at their faith.
Your problem and mine is to get behind the conventional
fronts that sit row upon row in the pews. [62]
We must penetrate the impersonality of modern living.
No mere academic acceptance of a message will suffice …
no mere academic message can ever meet the situation.
There must be that element of the personal in our
preaching that will reach the hearts of our people.
You remember when the prophet Nathan came to David,
to deal with the king's adultery and his murder of

Bathsheba's husband …

adroitly Nathan posed a hypothetical case, until the

king's indignation waxed hot.

Academically and on general principles he was indignant

at the very idea of a man who was so rich,

    stealing the one ewe lamb of a poorer neighbor.

And when David had exploded, "As the Lord liveth, the

man that hath done this thing shall surely die:

And he shall restore the lamb four-fold because he did

this thing, and because he had no pity …."[63]

Then Nathan, pointing the bony finger of accusation at

the king, said, "Thou art the man."[64]

Our preaching must have the quality of making each

person in the pew feel that he or she is the individual

immediately concerned.

The preacher must never forget that he himself is a

human being.

As we must bring our message down to the lives of the

men and women facing us …

as it must deal with their problems

          and passions

      and frailties,

so must we remember our own.

The preacher by his strength or weakness will give his

sermon color and bias.

James Black in his *The Mystery of Preaching* said,

"God has chosen us for His ambassadors.

In one sense God has just to take us as we are.

It is his glory that He can make us more than we are."[65]

It would certainly be presumptuous for me or anyone

else to indicate to you what you should preach.

He Who has called you into the ministry will place

upon your heart the message He wants you to proclaim.

And messages will come to you in many ways.

Who can tell how they will come?

George Buttrick says, "They are not found:

they come of themselves.

They jump from between the lines of the book you

are reading, though it may be a very secular book.

They look out at you through the mirror while you

are shaving.

They write themselves on the wall of the house

across the street.

They tremble in the glow of evening prayer.

How come sermons?"[66]

> How to the singer comes the song?
>
> How to the summer fields
>
> Come flowers? How yields
>
> Darkness to happy dawn? How doth the night
>
> Bring stars? ... "[67]

There are, however, certain things that I may be

permitted to say with regard to your message.

We shall never go wrong if we stick to the big

controlling fundamental truths.[68]

It is all very well for the preacher to select an

attractive title for his sermon[69]—especially if

his sermon topics are to appear in the "agony column"

on the church page ....[70]

And some men like Bernard Clausen, for example, have

a rare ability to give their sermons intriguing titles. [71]

We must not, however, prostitute our calling.

The preacher is never justified in donning cap and bells.

We must never be cheap.

And yet that is precisely the danger of trying to be

too original and to deal with sensational subjects

that go off at tangents.

Consider, for example, the needs of the people who will

come to hear you preach.

Use your imagination as you try to deal with the problems

that are most real to them.

There is a marriage that is almost on the rocks ….

    There is a son drinking heavily and breaking his

         mother's heart ….

There is a couple who are having a hard time financially …

and yonder is a young woman who has lost her baby ….

There is a son who is torn in loyalty between his wife and

    his mother …

and all over your congregation parents

              wives

          sisters

       and children who are anxious about

    men in service.

These are but a few of the commonest problems with which

our people are struggling.

How best can we deal with them?

Don't you see what they need?—Some assurance that God

is and that God cares.

They want to believe in prayer

and they want to find out how to pray,
to make God real …
they need guidance—how can they find it?
they need strength—how can it come?
What about sin?
What is sin?
How can they be rid of it?
How can they recover the peace of mind they used to have …
"the first fine careless rapture"[72] of Christian living?
Is there a second chance?
How can they start again?
Can this marriage be saved?
Can this boy who is drinking himself to death be
rescued?
How far does the providence of God extend to men in the
air corps … for the paratroops?
Can we believe that God will take care of them?
What does the Bible teach?
What has Christ to say?
Preach … preacher … the big controlling truths,[73]
for in them you have room
in them you can move
in them you have freedom
and in them you will find a message for which your
people are hungry.
If, when you write your sermons, you can see the
gleaming knuckles of a clenched fist …[74]
the lip that is bitten to keep back tears …
the troubled heart that is suffering because it
cannot forgive …

the spirit that has no joy because it has no love ….
If you can see the big tears that run down a mother's
face ….
If you can see these things—preach to them—

                  preach for them—

        and get down deep.[75]

But whatever you preach, be positive …

    preach only what you believe—and preach it as
if you believed it.[76]

It is not necessary to hit people over the head with
truth, but if we believe what we preach, there will
be an earnestness and a fervor generated by the
message itself that will bring conviction to the
hearts of the people before you.
In these days when terrible things are happening
in our world, we must have a tremendous gospel to
meet a tremendous need.
People are coming to us and saying, "I've lost my
faith in religion."
Widows of men lost in action whose hearts are in
agony …
who have been stampeded into the emptiness of despair.
They will have to be made to see that it is not
religion in which they have lost faith, but their
own theology.
The pattern of ideas that they had built up in their own
minds has been broken.
It is their understanding of religion that has given way.
There are many people in our congregations who had an
idea that just because they went to church

and said their prayers
and went through all the motions of conventional
religion that they and their loved ones would be entitled
to some special privileges, and that God would somehow
or other protect their men from the terrible things
that are happening to other men in battle.
Their particular theology into which they wove their
wishful thinking and their selfish love, believe that
God's providence would deliver their loved ones from
certain exigencies.
We have to point out to them that Christ never suggested
for a moment that His followers would be immune from the
troubles and the risks of life.
On the contrary, He made certain promises to all who would
come after Him ….
He promised them peace—not peace in the world around
them, but peace inside their own hearts.
He promised them joy—not that they would always be
surrounded by happiness, but that they would be able to
find a joy in sorrow ….
And he promised them trouble.
Jesus never blinked at facts, and He would not for a
moment have any of His followers blink at facts.
He did not promise to rescue His followers from trouble,
but to deliver them in the midst of trouble.
Many of our people had made a sort of charm of their
theology—a good-luck piece …
a sort of theological rabbit's foot …
as long as their loved ones are safe—their theology works,
but there was no connection between their theology and

the well-being of their loved ones.

It was pure coincidence

Their faith was in their theology rather than in their

religion.

Religion is not a way of getting God on your side

so that you can be protected from the world ....

Religion is rather a power that enables you to live in

harmony with God and your fellowmen in the world as it is.

True religion is realistic. It faces the facts of life.

The things it believes are not dependent upon chance

happenings.

They are not changed by whatever happens in the world

or by the exigencies of peace or of war.

It is these big, central truths that remain unshaken

and unaffected, that we must preach.

As I have said before, I would not for a moment presume

to suggest what you should preach—that is the

function of the Holy Spirit.

Yet, in a creedal church—and you have the Augsburg

Confession[77], even as we adopt the Westminster Confession[78]—

We are committed to certain great truths.

We are not free, as others might be, to choose a

subject just because it interests us ....

Nor are we free to expound from our pulpits what we

as individuals might think the meaning of the Scriptures

to be.

We have a certain framework for our message.

We have a certain theology.

Theology seeks to express the body—the essential body—

of Christian belief in clear and systematic form,
and so it uses the tools of logic
                        and language
            and the materials of faith
                        philosophy
            and the Scriptures to erect
        its structure.
Preaching seeks to gain adherence to that faith in
personal commitment and consecration, and therefore
it uses the tools of a witnessing personality.
It erects no structure,
It dictates no formula.
It seeks only to induce
                to compel
        to draw other personalities by its witness
to the power of the word of God.
The thing which makes preaching effective is the power
generated by the Word of God in the human heart translating
  belief and faith into action.
As guides for his message in time of war, let the preacher
consider the things that are happening in the world
and the experiences of his people as they deal with them
and are affected by them.
The Church has a message for today which can ring with all
the confidence and assurance of the prophets of old.
In normal peace times, the pulpit emphasis is usually on
purity and sanctification.
In time of war, we turn to the doctrine of justification.
Here is God using nations as instruments of His judgment,

just as He has always done.

It was His revelation to Habakkuk that He would use the
Assyrians for His own purposes that so shocked the
prophet ….

So God today can use Hitler.[79]

And the preacher can find comfort as well as warning in
the fact that God has not abdicated His throne, and that
His plans and purposes are not at the mercy of any
screaming dictator or any goddess from the sun.

It may well be that the Church is even now in the birth-
throes of a new conception of the providence.

The witness of Pastor Niemöller in Germany[80]

    of Bishop Berggrav in Norway[81]

has stirred many of us to believe that the throbbing,
vital heart of the Church today is not in its seminaries
nor in its cathedrals

    nor in Bishop's houses …

but in jails

      in concentration camps

            and prisons.

It is to be found, I sincerely believe, in the new
conviction that has come to the men and women who
in bitter cold, and in defiance of the Nazi storm
troopers and the Gestapo, could sing with tears
streaming down their faces ….[82]

    "Ein' feste Burg ist unser Gott"

If I may be bold enough to suggest that this emphasis
on the doctrine of justification should be one element

of our war-time preaching, it seems to me naturally
to suggest another, namely, the communion of the saints.
Although millions of us have repeated with devout
regularity the words of The Apostles Creed, this doctrine
is only now beginning to dawn upon the Christian
conscience ....
    "I believe in the communion of saints."[83]
One world indeed it is. The war has shrunk it.
The airplane and the radio have annihilated time and
distance ....[84]
and the tragedy is that our vision
                our faith
        and our love have not expanded
as our world has contracted.
We must not hate.
We know that as Christians we must not hate.
Are you not disturbed by the knowledge that there is
in America a great deal of hate ....
Negroes are hated
    Jews are hated
        Japs are hated[85]
labor union leaders are hated by management
and some in management are hated by labor ...
there is hate in our politics
    hate all around us.
The Christian nations are being set an example by
the most Christian government among the United Nations.
namely, the government of China
The Chiang Kai-Sheks have said for themselves and

said to their people that they will not and must not

hate the Japanese.[86]

When we realize that they, in their own private devotions,

are praying for the Japanese as well as their own people,

we catch something of the spirit that was in Christ.

Another element that must have a place in our preaching

in wartime is a real and sincere emotion.

The gospel we have to preach is emotion at its highest …

and that is the message our people are hungry for in this

time of their deepest need.

The criticism has often been levelled at the Presbyterian

Church that it is so cold …

and the dignity that Presbyterians have come to expect

in their services has often been a Frigidaire in which

we made ice cubes of our emotion.[87]

I would not say that we have become "icely faultless and

splendidly nil"[88] but these are days in which tears are

not very far away from any one of us …

and sorrow is weeping softly in many a heart.

But what could be more emotional than the idea of a

suffering God?

How could we speak of the cross without emotion?

Where is there a more profound expression of the highest

emotion than in John 3:16?[89]

We will be preaching a lot about the cross in these days

for we need to be reassured of God's love and everlasting

pity.

Now this does not demand that the preacher introduce a

falsetto, or a tremolo into a voice.

The ministerial tone only makes a man ridiculous …

the strained, pathetic effect does not impress people save
perhaps with a sense of shame that they should be exposed
to such a vulgar display.

"The most passionate music is not the most luscious;
a great violinist scorns the tremolo.
Beethoven speaks more quietly but no less intensely
than Tchaikovsky;
pathos is not limited to symphonies labeled 'Pathètique.'
The classic lyrics are chiseled understatements
of emotion."

—Irwin Edman.[90]

There was a time when the congregations of America were
emotionally "punch drunk" by these themes …
the death-bed illustrations

the mournful voice

and the mock tears form a religious framework which
has become empty to most people today—even repulsive,
so that they shy away from it.
Let us, as preachers, be sensitive to our message that
we shall be moved by it …
and if we sincerely feel compassion

or sorrow

indignation or conviction, they will all be
reflected in our expression and tone.
If we live our words, we shall live their meaning.
C. E. Montague, in his novel *Rough Justice* tells
of a little English boy named Bron who goes to church
for the first time with his governess.[91]
He watched with interest every part of the service

and then the preacher climbs into the high pulpit and
Bron hears him give out a piece of terrible news.
It is about a brave and kind man Who was nailed to
a cross, ferociously hurt a long time ago, and feeling
a dreadful pain even now, because there was something
not done that He wanted them all to do.
Little Bron thought the preacher was telling the
story because a lot of people were there, and they would
do something about it.
Bron is on the edge of the pew and wonders why, if
such an injustice has been done to an innocent man,
no one does anything about it.
But he sits quietly and decides that after the service
someone will do something about it.
Little Bron weeps, but nobody else seems at all
upset by it.
The service over, the people walk away as if nothing
remarkable had happened.
As Bron leaves the church he is trembling.
His governess looks at him and says: "Bron, don't
take it to heart, someone will think you are queer."[92]
But Calvary is the story of a Man who took things
terribly to heart.
It is the privilege and the penalty of the preacher
that he must take the gospel terribly to heart.
He must take terribly to heart the things that are
happening in this world
     and in the lives of his people,
so must the man called by God proclaim the message

God has given

    laid upon his heart

    sent rustling round the whispering gallery of his soul.

In the broad sense, the world is full of preachers.
In fact the fraternity seems to be growing.
I have been reading lately some fine sermons in the
editorial pages of our newspapers, and have been stirred
by the sermonic quality of messages where one would least
expect to find them—in the pages of a pictorial
magazine.[93]
The press is one of the most influential preachers of
our time.
You will find preachers among the poets

        and the playwrights

      and occasionally a motion picture will preach a
sermon and leave an impression in the minds and hearts
of a movie audience that would be quite beyond most
of us.
But in the narrow sense, our call is different.
We have been called to serve a particular congregation
and to be to its members a pastor

        a preacher

      a prophet

     a counselor

  and a friend.
If at times the task seems too much for us, as it does
now and then—it were well to remember the words of
Christ, "Ye have not chosen me, but I have chosen you
and ordained you that you should go and bring forth

fruit, and that your fruit should remain."[94]
That ought to be enough for a hundred doubts and fears.
Nevertheless, discouragements will come in a melancholy
procession and sit down in their dejected rows in the
chapels of our hearts.[95]
The times will come—and for me they come on Sunday
nights—when a sense of utter futility will sweep over
your very soul.
If your experience is at all like mine, it will not be
the empty pews that will depress you …
nor the inane chatter of the people who speak to you
after the service is over …
when instead of going home with serious purpose
    or going out into the night with shining eyes
           and quivering lip
they linger instead to reveal by the things they
talk about how inhospitable their hearts and minds
have been to the message you have just delivered …
No, it will not be these things so much as your
feeling of the inadequacy of your message.
It will come surging in upon you when you are utterly
spent—as you ought to be after a service—that
somehow you have missed a great opportunity.
You will think of the things you might have said,
and you will be sorry for some things you said—
which, like horses with bits in their teeth
broke away from your wiser judgment.
At such times, gentlemen, we are at once humbled
and comforted ….
"Without me ye can do nothing …."[96]

These words will indict us for our reliance upon our
own cleverness and oratory …
and for our comfort, there will come the words of
Paul, "for it pleased God by the foolishness of
preaching to save them that believed."[97]
The constant miracle and the glory of our call lies
in the fact that Christ has used preaching and will
use your preaching and mine for the up-building of
the kingdom of God.
The chief purpose of the ministry is to win men and
women to the way of life which Christ taught.
That in my opinion is more definitive than the vague
phrase "to preach the gospel."
Although the preacher's function may be stated in a
hundred different ways, it must in essence persuade
men and women to discover and to do the will of God
in their everyday lives

Dr. Peter Marshall preaching to over 10,000 people at the Easter Service
Fort Lincoln Heights, Washington, D.C.,
April 5, 1942

III.

———

LIGHTS!

The Vision

"There can be no logic to prove the spiritual.
There can only be the prophet's opening of a
window in the hope that clay-shuttered eyes and
sin-darkened sight may find a magic casement looking
out upon the mountains of God."[98]
The problem of the poet
                    the playwright
         the artist
      the prophet
And the preacher has always been to make people
see.[99]
Somehow we must rekindle the imaginations of our
people, for spiritual perception must be personally
apprehended.
One can no more impart his idea of God
            his vision of Christ
      his understanding of the kingdom to someone
else than he can sift gold dust from the butterfly's
wings.
Spiritual appreciations are felt, not fingered.

They are caught like germs of the soul, not like
fly-balls which the preacher bats out from the
pulpit.
We are, in this sophisticated twentieth century, very
weak in imagination, in spite of the great development
in the art of pictorial advertising that makes its
appeal by way of suggestion …
and suggestion is an appeal to the imagination
rather than to the will.
Children enter into a new world through the
portals of imagination.
The child can take a broom stick, and straddling it,
by his own peculiar magic, can make its one wooden
leg change into four galloping hoofs …
and its straw become a mane whistling through every
wind.[100]
Every night millions of men and women like ourselves
sit in picture houses and are carried away in their
imaginations to live other lives
    and to be other people for two or three hours.
Give people a picture and it will remain clearly
etched in recollection when the homily has become a
blur.
George Bernard Shaw in his play, "St. Joan," makes
Captain Robert de Baudricourt, question Joan of Arc
who says,
    "I hear voices telling me what to do.
    They come from God."
The captain says in scorn: "They come from your
    imagination."

Then Joan says, "Of course, that is how the messages
of God come to us."[101]
You will see this principle at work in the teachings
of Jesus.
A lawyer comes to him to ask about the way of life.
Jesus answers the question—as He so often did—by
asking another, "What is written in the law?"
"How readest thou?"[102]
As if to say, "the law is your profession—you ought
to know."
But the lawyer, undaunted, answers smoothly,
"Thou shalt love the Lord thy God with all
thy heart, and with all thy soul and with
all thy mind, and thy neighbor as thyself."[103]
There was a finality in the voice of Jesus,
"Continue to do that, and thou shalt live."[104]
Then follows the typical legalistic question:
"Who is my neighbor?"[105]
How would Jesus define a neighbor?
Was a Samaritan a neighbor?
Was a publican—or a sinner?
Now Jesus did not supply the lawyer with a list of
people who might be neighbors.
He did not indicate those to whom this rule would
not apply.
Instead, He told a story.
He lifted the question out of the atmosphere of
controversy and set it down on a dangerous road
in Palestine.

The story lays its constraint on the conscience of
mankind in every age.
It was the story of the Good Samaritan.
At the end of the tale there was only one thing
left to say, "Go thou and do likewise."[106]
It was a picture of how we are to interpret the
divine law—use your imagination.
Unless what the preacher says is real and vivid
to him, it will never be real or vivid to his
congregation.
If the lantern itself is unlit, it cannot throw a
picture on the screen for the audience, no matter
how beautiful, how true or accurate the picture
itself may be …
it will remain unillumined, dark and dead.
After rebuilding the entire context, the preacher
should be able to understand just what happened
in any particular situation.
He should possess and develop the faculty for
placing himself in the position of someone else—
to feel how he felt who wrote the narrative …
or how they felt who were his first readers.
In describing any particular incident, imagine
yourself there.
Even as you read the words, some picture must be
present in your mind.
if you describe what you see, others can be
transported into an experience of the event you
describe.

Let me illustrate what I mean.

What picture do you have in your mind as Moses

first appeared before Pharaoh?[107]

Moses walked forward over the tiled floor to where

Pharaoh sat on his stone throne with its huge

carved figures for arms.

Giant Nubian slaves stood behind him, working the

screens of palms that moved the humid air heavy with

exotic fragrance.

He blinked his eyes in the bright sunshine—so bright

that the shadows seemed to be etched in purple on the

floor.

He advanced slowly, aware of the inscriptions

      the frescoes

   the tiles

    and the very stones eloquent with

boastings and stories of conquest.

In the sharp shadows Pharaoh sat, a thinly veiled sneer

on his lips …

  his smooth chin cupped in one hand,

watching through half-shut eyes.

Moses felt the threat of the hanging draperies.

They were a dark red—as dark as blood drying in the

sand … and Moses remembered the color of it—for

he had seen Egyptian blood on the sand …

  and he shivered slightly.

He was impressed with the magnificence of the palace

court, and the sense of Pharaoh's power.

But he remembered that he had just come from an

audience with Jehovah—a power greater, he believed,

than Pharaoh's power … and he grew bold again.

His courage returned, and he thought of his commission.

He straightened up, until he looked Pharaoh right in

the eye without blinking, and he said simply, just as

it is written:

"Thus saith the Lord God of Israel, 'let My people go.'"[108]

The details of the picture can be gleaned from Bible

dictionaries,

    commentaries

        and the history books …

but your imagination must make the characters alive.

What about the scene in the porch of the Temple that

is sketched for us by John in his eighth chapter?[109]

Jesus is standing watching the people come in and

go out.

There are shadows in His eyes, and no man can tell

the thoughts that run through His mind.

A group surges forward to where He stands, pushing

their way through the morning worshippers.

He has seen them now … and turns to meet them.

His face is clouded suddenly, for a moment,

    and pain looks out from His eyes

        and He sighs.

Some Scribes and Pharisees thrust their way towards

Christ.

In the midst of them is a woman—being dragged

roughly by strong men whose faces are hard and stern.

They are pulling her along …

in their strong grip on her arms she winces with pain.

With all the strength of their contempt they

Throw her down at Jesus' feet.

Then they spew out their accusations …

in voices honed on hate they shout the vile names

reserved for such women who give their bodies

without giving their souls.

There are voices hot like scorching blasts from

a furnace, …

And others cold, as if they came from frozen hearts.

The woman shivers and moans as she listens.

Her head is bowed.…

    her face covered with her hands …

her hair is dishevelled, and falls over her shoulders

like a screen.

Her dress is torn and stained with the dust of the

streets along which they have dragged her.

An infinite sadness has settled on the face of Jesus,

as if the load of all the sin since the world began

has already been laid upon Him.

The hard faces that look down on her have no pity

in them, nor mercy.

These men weigh the stones they have picked up,

turning them round in their clawing hands …

running their fingers along the sharpest edge with

a horrible satisfaction.

Their shouting ceases as the calm penetrating look of

Christ travels round the circle … questioningly …

only to break out again as one of them shouts the

indictment.

The woman—whose name we do not know—is an adulteress.

They had caught her in the very act.

Her head sinks lower in the shame of it …

    the public accusation

 but it seems as if Jesus does not look at her at all ….

He is watching those men who try to hide the stones

they carry in their hands.

They are ready to throw them at the poor defenceless

creature on the ground.

They have appointed themselves her self-righteous

judges, and brought the woman to Christ—not for formal

trial … for they had already tried her …

but in order to get His expression of opinion on a

point of the Mosaic law, which might afterwards be

used against Him.

It was a trap for the Nazarene.

"Master … Moses in the law commanded us …

that such should be stoned: but what sayest Thou?"[110]

Either He had to condemn the woman—or release her.

If He condemned the woman … He would not be merciful

         and He said that He was merciful!

If He said that she should be stoned … he would be

    subject to Roman law for inciting to murder!

If He released the woman … He would be setting

aside the law of Moses,

and they could say that He was a blasphemous person,

who has broken the law.

In either case, they thought, He was trapped.

The dilemma was neatly framed.

But the dilemma of Justice—or Pardon—was no

great dilemma to Him Who solved it in the Incarnation.
Jesus detested adultery … but He also detested
hypocrisy.
What will He do?
All eyes are upon Him.
He stoops down … and with His finger He writes in
the dust.
He does not speak … just traces out in the sand
characters that slowly take the form of words
written there on the floor.
This is the only time we know of His writing anything …
and no one has ever known what he wrote.
If He wrote the word adulteress—the word that they
were shouting so loudly … it does not stay long …
for an eddy of wind swirls round the pillars of the
Temple porch and covers it with sand.
He looks at them … steadily … with eyes that
never blink … and then He speaks,

    "He that is without sin among you …

      let him first cast a stone at her."[111]

He steps back a few paces … and stooping again,
continues to write … and this time the winds do not
blow the words away.
His keen glance rests upon the accusers one by one …
and He writes … there in the sand at their feet …

        word after word …

They watch His finger … fascinated … as it
travels up and down … making letters that the
wind could not blow away …

and which men could not read without trembling.
Some of the Scribes and Pharisees have begun to leave.
There is a deathly silence … as bearded men look
over the shoulders of their friends … and watch …
Christ looks up into the faces … and sees into the
yesterdays that lie hidden in the pools of memory and
conscience. He sees into their very hearts.
According to ancient tradition, His finger traces the
word "Thief" … and one of the Pharisees hurries away ….
He looks up at another of them . . . holds His gaze for
a moment … and then the finger moves again …
this time to form the word "Murderer" … whereupon
from the circle a man turns and runs from the thinning
group …
and there is a thud of a stone falling on the pavement.
Not many remain … those who do are fascinated and
afraid … as that finger writes … slowly …
     like the wheels of judgment …
slowly the record is traced in the dust …
and the story of their sin is marked in the sand.
One by one they go … shuffling off into the crowded
street to lose themselves in the multitudes.
"He that is without sin among you …
     let him first cast a stone at her."[112]
But the adulteress could not have been unfaithful
     had a man not tempted her …
the thief would not steal … were the rich more generous.
The murderer would not kill were he not driven to
desperation …

there would be no harlots if men had no evil passions.

The guiltless alone have the right to judge others.

"Let the sinless among you be her executioner," He had

said! But there are no sinless on earth.

No stone had been thrown … but they lie around her

on the pavement.

The stillness is broken only by the sobbing of the

woman.

None of the actors in the scene remained but two—

 the criminal … and the Judge …

 sin … and Holiness!

No longer was any voice crying for her blood …

nor any hand uplifted for her death.

There was now no one with her but Innocence …

the only One Who might have had the right to throw

a stone … but no stone was in His hand.

Lifting His eyes from the floor …. He said to her,

after the impressive pause that always precedes

the speech of God:

 "Woman, where are those thine accusers?

  Hath no man condemned thee?"[113]

And she answered: "No man, Lord."[114]

That is all the woman says from the beginning to the end.

She had no excuse for her conduct …

no attempt to justify what she had done …

The Lord Jesus … looking at her …

seeing the tear-stained cheek and the lashes

wet with tears …

seeing further … into her heart … said unto her:

"Neither do I condemn thee....

Go ... and sin no more!"[115]

"What a strange verdict for Day to pass on Night![116]

For Virtue to pass on Vice!

Here was the love of God at work.

Here was Divine mercy in action, saying to sinners

of that day and of ours:

"You are black, but I send you to fountains of

cleansing.

You come from shadows ... but I send you to the Sun ...

I despise your sin ... but I love you, the sinner ...

I condemn what you have done ... but I forgive you ...

I blame you for your rotten past ... but I wipe it

out forever ...

You are unworthy to live ... but by My Grace, you

shall live to be worthy.

Go now ... and sin no more!"

And His soft voice was like candle-light at twilight ...

like a prayer in the evening ...

or the fragrance of a rose in a sick-room ...

like music of a birdsong after a storm ...

it was medicine of mercy for a sin-sick heart.

There is no further sound.

If she breathed her gratitude ... it is so soft that

only He heard it ...

or perhaps she spoke in that language of the heart

that only God can read.

Maybe He smiled upon her ... a slow, sad smile of One

Who knew that He had to pay the price of that absolution.

Maybe His head was bowed ... and His fingers wrote again

in the dust … tracing the outline of a cross …
or drawing the shape of a bleeding, broken heart.
As we watch the woman, her face lights up …
shadows are fading and lines smoothed out …
the circles under her eyes disappear …
she raises her head … and looks up.
Things are different for her—now
She will never be the same again, for she has looked
into the eyes of the Nazarene, and her own eyes are
glowing like altar lights …
shining like stars …
for she has seen God!
She is a new woman.
It seemed as if her old self had died huddled there
and had been born all over again.
"Go … and sin no more!"
It rings in her ears
it whispers in her heart
it challenges her soul
it calls like a bugle
it gives her strength and courage.
Broken—she has been mended in the workshop of God's
mercy.
In the Gospel according to Luke, you will read these
words in chapter 19:[117]
"And Jesus entered and passed through Jericho.
And behold there was a man named Zacchaeus,
which was the chief among the publicans,
and he was rich.

And he sought to see Jesus who he was; and
could not for the press, because he was
little of stature.
And he ran before, and climbed up into a
sycamore tree to see Him: for he was to
pass that way."[118]
There in a few strokes, gentlemen, you have a picture—
a drama of human interest—what do you see?
Jesus was passing through Jericho on His way to
Jerusalem, and as usual He was in the center of
a crowd …
and His disciples were following behind.
As the procession made its way through the town,
Zacchaeus was attracted by the noise and, learning
from some passerby who shouts over his shoulder as
he runs, that Jesus of Nazareth—this itinerant
Teacher of Whom he had heard such glowing tales …
was actually passing through Jericho ….
He goes eagerly to see for himself this Great
Galilean Who had taken the whole country-side by storm.
He must be a big man—thought Zacchaeus—a man
of broad sympathy and understanding …
imagine calling another tax-gatherer, Matthew,
to be one of His disciples!
Zacchaeus quickened his step until he too was
hurrying.
It did not take him long to find the crowd—going
right down Main street ….
He darted down a side street to come into the main
highway ahead of the procession.

The crowd as it surged past him, caught him up in
its tumult and carried him forward.
But Zacchaeus could not see Jesus.
Try as he might—it seemed to be impossible.
I can imagine him standing on his tiptoes, craning
his neck ….
making funny little jumps
        becoming more and more excited
                and exasperated
            and impatient
 responding to the enthusiasm of the mob …
growing desperate as the crowd moved along.
Again and again Zacchaeus tried to see over the
shoulders of his taller fellows …
and he keeps bobbing up and down—like a painted
rubber ball.
Zacchaeus suddenly realized that he wanted to see
Jesus very much.
What was He like?
He knew men who had been with Him, and who were different.
Somehow he wanted to be different too.
                He forgot himself.
But he could not see Jesus.
There were two things that prevented him from
realizing his ambition in this respect.
First—the crowd was great. There were too many
people between him and Christ.
And in the second place Zacchaeus was small of stature.
                He was a little man.

Now that was no fault of his.

You can't blame Zacchaeus for his lack of inches.

Zacchaeus was afraid that he might not catch a glimpse

of Jesus after all.

Well, what should he do?

    What did he do?

First, he left the crowd.

That was a splendid move—it was not hard for

Zacchaeus because in a sense he was never with the

crowd. He was always apart—a very lonely man.

Well, in leaving the crowd, Zacchaeus overcame

the first obstacle—but still he had not seen Jesus ….

He still had to do something about his lack of inches ….

So he ran forward a little distance and climbed

up into the branches of a sycamore tree.

This tree never attains any great height …

    And its foliage is sparse ….

But it was the only thing available ….

And the truth was—Zacchaeus did not think very

carefully about the second move …

the idea had suddenly come to him, and he acted

upon it on the impulse.

It takes a big emotion to make men forget their dignity.

The picture is almost grotesque as we see Zacchaeus

perched in the stunted tree like an overgrown,

        gaily dressed crow.

By this time the procession was drawing near …

in just a few minutes it would pass along the road

and maybe Jesus would even walk in the shadow cast

by the tree.

Ah … there He is … that must be He …

right in the center ….

Zacchaeus noted that the face was kind without being

weak …

he noted the grace of His walk

How He held Himself …

he saw His gestures—they were different somehow …

no wonder He has made such an impression—he thought …

And, while he feasted his eyes on Jesus, he chuckled

softly to himself as he thought how surprised the

crowd would be if they could see him.

But the crowd was not looking into the boughs of

the tree.

"I will never be noticed up here," he laughed softly,

"Nobody will ever think of looking up as they pass

by and, besides, if they do look, they may not

recognize me for I am partly hidden by the leaves."

Zacchaeus hoped that he would not be discovered.

They would not understand—they would laugh at him

and mock him ….

They would jeer and laugh to see the rich man of the

custom house perched up in a sycamore tree.

He would be terribly embarrassed.

Jesus was now right beneath the tree, and, suddenly—

He stopped.

Zacchaeus felt his heart thumping against his ribs.

Why had He stopped right there?

Surely he had not been discovered.

No, He would move on again in a moment.

These thoughts passed each other like lightening in
his mind, and then—
Jesus looked up …. He looked right into the tree,
	right at Zacchaeus …
and the eyes of the two men met.
But Jesus was smiling ….
His eyes were twinkling with merriment ….
Jesus was laughing at him.
My, how Zacchaeus was embarrassed!
Great beads of perspiration stood out on his forehead
as the thought spread into his warped skull …
	"He is looking at me, He has seen me."
And then Zacchaeus heard a name spoken—it was his name.
"My imagination is playing me tricks—no, it couldn't
be my name—He doesn't know me ….
He has never seen me before—besides, I'm a publican,
I have no friends …
it can't be my name this Galilean has spoken."
But sure enough, there it was again, and there could be
no mistake this time:
"Zacchaeus, make haste and come down for today I must
abide at thy house."
And while the crowd gaped in astonishment and curiosity,
he jumped down from the boughs of the tree, and with
undisguised joy, his eyes beaming with a new light …
	his face with an expression it never before had known,
he led the way to his house.
Imagination, gentlemen, a sanctified imagination,
		an active mind dedicated to God,
	a mind that can see things …

is a great instrument in the hands of the Holy Spirit.[119]
The greatest adventure story in the world is a
book called "The Acts of the Apostles."
In this absorbing story you will follow Paul, the traveler,
who early in his missionary life gave proof of his
sound practical mind …

    and that fine strategy of Christian statesmanship …
by deciding that he could best spread the seed of
Christianity by preaching in the large cities,

    the centers of the Roman trade routes.
He sought out the boom towns,

        the junctions of the great roads,

          the ports where ships from
strange places let down their anchors.
And so it is when we read the story we can half close
our eyes and see swinging along the roads that
were the pride of Imperial Rome …

            bands of jugglers
and dancing girls on their way to Antioch, the Paris
of the East,

    cohorts on the march

        merchants from Baghdad and Damascus

          with their silks and perfumes,

            itinerant Greek philosophers

        gladiators

    men with caged beasts for the circus,
and pagan priests begging their way with a god in

            a tent.
Somewhere in that crowd,

    symbols of the old world and the new—

a Roman senator traveling in state on some
imperial mission …

    and, humbly and on foot, a Christian on a still
greater mission—Paul went with a staff in his
hand …

        to turn the Roman Empire as on a hinge,
      to turn the world upside down,
with a message of a Saviour Who was nailed to a tree.
We see him standing on the deck of a Mediterranean
coaster, as he must have done many times, straining
with those dim eyes of his to see the distant shore.
Paul must have known the grey light,
        the last star,
          the cold wind,
        the smell of beasts and tar,
      the swing of the mast against the sky,
      the hiss of the water,
        and the creaking of the spars,
the long sudden roll of the ship, as he embarked on
yet another perilous journey to take the Good News
farther across the world.
He must have wondered, as he stood there in the first
troubled light of dawn, what new dangers and
privations awaited him below the restless horizon.
Did he ever hear a voice crying out of the windy sea,
"And ye shall be hated of all men for My name's
sake; but he that endureth to the end shall be saved.
But when they persecute you in this city, flee ye to
another …?"[120]

Would he have reflected that he now, above all men,
surely knew what that meant?
During the weekdays Paul worked at his trade as a
tentmaker.
We see him in Corinth, squatting on the floor of a
tiny house, with his friend Aquilla,
 stitching on a sail cloth spread between them.
The declining sun casts the sharp shadows of olive
trees across their work
    and the air floating in through the open door
is heavy with the fragrance of pomegranates
 as the two friends talk of the newest problem in
the struggling little church,
    or Paul asks eager questions about Rome and
looks up as he says wistfully: "I must go to Rome …
                somehow …
          sometime …
       I must preach in Rome."
After the fires of the blood-red Mediterranean sunset
have died out and the soft Syrian night has laid
down a quilt of purple shadows,
    when the tentmakers have finished their work for
the day, we can imagine men and women—just a few—
        leaving the crowds in the streets,
      softly crossing moonlit squares where
the stone faces of gods and emperors smile in the
 flickering light from braziers,
              and disappearing
into the narrow streets that lead to the Potter's
quarter and the house of Justus.

Paul is there to greet them,
> and Silas,
> > and Timothy,
> and Aquila,
> and Priscilla.

A passer-by, hearing the sound of voices, might have
glanced in to see a little man …
> with eyebrows that joined,
> > and a nose somewhat hooked.
> standing in the feeble lamplight,
> > his short figure casting a grotesque
 shadow on the white-washed walls,
> > his face alive with earnestness and
tenderness,
> telling the simple converts gathered
around him the story of Someone Who said:
> "Do this in memory of Me."[121]

When Paul thus becomes real to you in your imagination,
you can make him live to your people,
 and as Paul lives,
> > his words will whisper themselves
in haunting meaning to men and women of the twentieth
century who discover with a thrill
> that there is a timeless element in the Word of God.

In the realm of the imagination, no preacher, by
taking thought, can add one cubit unto the stature
of the narrative itself.[122]
> > but he can fill in,
> with detail and self-projection,

some life,

color,

and action to the story

He must see the picture for himself, and reconstruct

it in his own mind.

It must be made to live.

The characters must be set in motion.

When they come to life in the preacher's imagination

then all he has to do is to describe what he sees.

He must keep the essential details true to the

scriptures,

and consult maps,

Bible dictionaries,

history books and other references

to make sure that his context is accurate.

Pictorial preaching is the most effective because "it

is easier to get at the average mind by a picture than

by an idea.

An Arab proverb puts it this way:

"He is the best

speaker who can turn the ear into an eye."[123]

Preaching on characters in the Bible,

or incidents in their lives,

demands pictorial preaching,

with imaginative treatment and in a dramatic

setting,

"It is a piece of life …

a film from the world's big drama …"[124]

a newsreel from the Scriptures.

You must sketch your situation as you were painting it.

For your colors you have words …

    your sermon outline provides the lines of your

               picture.

For your brushes you have gestures and the

modulations of your voice.

For your shadows and highlights you have your

own expression and the tone of your voice.[125]

Now if words are to be our colors, we must see to it

that we select the right shade.

Dr. George A. Buttrick, himself a master of words,

 said in his *Jesus Came Preaching* ….

    "There are Anglo-Saxon words of one syllable …

        (staccato words like "sin"

            haunting words like "home",

               ultimate words like "God")

that grapple the heart with hooks of steel.

"Let the long sequences of juicy adjectives be cut

away ….

    One adjective is better than six

        and none is often better than one."[126]

Some of the sublimest things in our English

language have been said with very simple words.

Think of the language of the King James version

        of the Bible.

Think of the speeches of Abraham Lincoln.[127]

    There you have simple words with a power and

appeal that ornate language could never have.

It is well worth the time and trouble it takes

sometimes to find the right word with the desired

shade of meaning.

The use of the right word,

            the exact word,

    is the difference between a pencil with a sharp

point, and a thick crayon.

You have achieved good style in pulpit speech when

no word of your sentence structure could be changed

without changing your meaning.

Good strong robust Anglo-Saxon words are most useful,

            and, as guides to the right word,

      there is no substitute for time and thought,

and the painstaking consulting of the dictionary

          and a good thesaurus.[128]

The only purpose of this word painting is to enable

your hearers to see what you see …

        to feel what you feel.

As John Ruskin has said:

  The greatest thing a human soul ever does in

  this world is to see something, and tell what

  He saw in a plain way.[129]

  Hundreds of people can talk for one who can think,

  but thousands can think for one who can see.

    To see clearly is poetry,

        prophecy

      and religion … all in one."

There is your task, gentlemen,

    To see clearly,

and to tell what you see in a plain way.

Dr. Peter Marshall with his 5" x 7" sermon notebook.

IV.

CAMERA!

The Method

Paul speaks to all of us men who are called to
preach the Word of God when he exhorts young
Timothy:

> "Study to show thyself approved unto God,
> a workman that needeth not to be ashamed,
> rightly dividing the word of truth."[130]

The Bible is our text-book

It is our final authority, for we believe it to

be "the only infallible rule of faith and practice."[131]

Hence the importance of our correctly interpreting

its message.

The providence of God and the heroism of our

fathers have preserved the Bible for us today.

All of us have access to it in our own language;

some of us, in the original languages.

Some of it is so plain that it may be understood

by the smallest child;

some of it is too deep for the wisest men.

Most of it can be understood by those who are

willing to pay the price for true interpretation.

The preacher must be guarded against misinterpretation
because he is dealing with the Word of God.
It is a fearful responsibility that rests upon the
interpreter.
The Bible is the most important book known to
mankind.
It has been the source of life and light for
untold millions.
Truly indeed is the Word of God "quick and powerful,
 and sharper than any two-edged sword,
     piercing even to the dividing asunder of soul
and spirit, and of the joints and marrow,
and is a discerner of the thoughts and intents of
the heart."[132]
The author of the epistle to the Hebrews would
make the message of the Scriptures no dead letter!
It is rather charged with power.
As God's all-seeing scrutiny should deter from
wrong-doing. His word written by inspired men, will
indict them as well as give them comfort and hope.
As the Scriptures principally teach "what man is to
believe concerning God, and what duty God requires of
man,"[133] it behooves the preacher to be a careful
interpreter.
What he expounds of the Word of God will affect the
religious thinking of his hearers …
and he must not be a false teacher, subverting the
revealed Word of God.
Moreover, he must make the truth live in applications
to his day.

There are such things as principles of interpretation,
and with them, the preacher must be familiar.
He must, like a master-craftsman, know how to use his
tools.
The Bible must speak its own truth to us—not the
message we would like to hear.
We dare not come to the Bible to find confirmation
for our own ideas or theories …
but rather to discover what the Bible teaches, and to
govern ourselves thereby.

(1) The first basic principle of interpretation is that
every particular writing must be interpreted in the
light of its own context.
The meaning of any portion of sacred writing can be
revealed only when the original context has been
reconstructed.
It was that original context that gave the writing its
meaning in the first place,
and if the original context be restored, then, and
only then, the original meaning will be revealed.
There is a wealth of meaning in the term "context."
It is made up of many elements.
Suppose, for example, two thousand years from now,
some archeologist were to dig up a spark plug
from the plains of Kansas …
or in some excavations on the site of the ancient
American city of Detroit.
This mysterious thing might be properly identified

as a means whereby the primitive people of the
first half of the twentieth century exploded the vapors
of gasoline by means of an electric spark.
But it would have to be determined whether it were
used in an automobile
    or in an airplane
     or a tank
      or a jeep.
What was it designed to do?
 Who designed it?
  What was its function?
 How did its invention affect American life
and culture?
Journeys that had taken days were made possible in
a matter of hours.
Distance was annihilated.
A social and economic revolution had been made possible.
All these questions would face the man with the
spade, who had dug up this curiosity.
He would find that the context had many sides.
We must restore, where we can, all the elements of
the original context, which I would break into five
parts—namely, the grammatical
  the historical
 the literary
 the logical
and the psychological.
(a) In considering the grammatical context, we must
let the words of the original language speak for

themselves, for the author in using these particular
words had a particular reason.
They were selected because they conveyed exactly
the idea he wished to convey.[134]
So, therefore, the interpreter must endeavor to know
as much as possible about the vocabulary and the
grammar of the language in which the message is written.
It is very difficult for any translation to bring out
exactly all the fine shades of meaning in the original—
so that the preacher who knows neither Hebrew nor Greek
must always be somewhat at a disadvantage, although
there are available to him excellent translations
and discussions as to meaning by scholars who have made
a study of the original languages.
Our task is to get at the author's meaning ...
and we can get it only as we discover the meaning of
the words he used.
For example, in the sixth chapter of Paul's epistle
to the Galatians, you will find the interpreter's
problem presented in the apparent contradiction in the
second and fifth verses.
In the Authorized version you read in verse two:

> "Bear ye one another's burden, and so fulfill
> the law of Christ ...."[135]

But in verse five you read:

> "For every man shall bear his own burden."

What then?

> Is Paul contradicting himself?

How can we bear one another's burdens if each is
required to bear his own?

How then is this apparent contradiction to be resolved?

When the grammatical context is restored, you discover

that in the Greek text two different words [for burden] are used.

In the second verse, it is the word βάρη.[136]

While in the fifth verse it is the word φορτίον.

Now Paul certainly used two different words in order to

convey two different shades of meaning.

The root of the word βάρη suggests a picture of a

traveller trudging along life's highway with a burden

slung over his shoulder.

The idea is that with regard to the handicaps

some people have to carry we should be helpful.

There are things in life that oppress and make

life hard.

As regards to them, the Christian must ever lend

a helping hand to his fellow-wayfarer.

But the word φορτίον conveys a different picture.

Here it means equipment

            accoutrement …

  it suggests those things physical

          material

       intellectual

    or cultural with which a person

may be endowed. They constitute his own personal

responsibility. He is responsible for them and must

give an account.

In that sense, every man must bear his own

responsibility.

With regard to his sin, he cannot blame it on
another, even although Adam tried to do just that
and all the sons of Adam are willing to attempt
it until this day.
But even as the soldier is held personally responsible
for the equipment issued to him, so are we all to
give an account to God Who hath freely given us all
things.
Now I suggest to you that no ingenuity or originality
could reveal the apostle's meaning were not the
grammatical context in this case completely restored.
(b) Each of the books in the Bible was written in a
particular historical background, and for the purpose
of meeting a definite historical situation.
Before we can understand the author's message, we
must ask what were the circumstances at the time
of the writing ...
and what were the circumstances of those to whom
he wrote?
What was the political situation?
    What is the date of the writing?
        and the social environment?
What particular occasion called forth the writing?
Without this element of the context—what the author
wrote might seem to have an entirely different meaning—
or no meaning at all.
(c) The literary context also must be determined.
In what form did the author write?
It may not always be easy to determine the form since
the Bible contains so many—there is prose

and poetry
and allegory
and parable
and satire
and metaphor
and simile
and apocalypse.

We must deal fairly with the form used.

May I in some trepidation try to illustrate what I mean?

In the book of Genesis, we read:

> "And the Lord God formed man of the
>
> dust of the ground, and breathed into
>
> his nostrils the breath of life; and
>
> man became a living soul."[137]

The Bible is not always what it seems to those who

read it in the great prose of the English version,[138]

or indeed in any of the conventional versions.

These words "God formed man from [sic]the dust of the ground"

may be argued by some to be poetry …

and indeed poetry they are.

It is a poetic phrase …

and yet we know in the light of anthropology that they

are also literally true.

You can see in the anthropological department of any

good museum, laid out in little saucers neatly labelled,

the constituent elements of the human body.[139]

There is so much phosphorus

silicon
iron
carbon

lime

        water … and so on …

enough phosphorus, it is said, to dip the heads

of one thousand matches …

enough iron to make half a dozen ten-penny nails …

enough lime to white-wash a chicken-coop …

      and so on …

and that—says modern science—is the human body.

But is not that exactly what the Book says? …

That "God formed man," that is, Adam—that organism

so named to distinguish it from the organism of a

cow or a dog—"from the dust of the ground" …

of mineral substances … exactly.

And then the Bible proceeds, "God breathed into

    him the breath of life and he became

    a living soul."[140]

In other words, something was added to this

organism that made it different from all other

organisms …

and that which was added is called "the breath of

life."

Another poetic phrase, you will observe, but it

comes from the same root as the word which is used

to describe the spirit of God brooding over the face of the waters.

Thus man was in-breathed with that which made him

like God.

He was given a soul …

and a soul is a spiritual substance in which

certain attributes adhere …

the attributes generally being described as the

attributes of intellect

       sensibility

          and will.

In dealing with poetry, we have to remember that

the poet has a message which he sends singing in

words that dance, but it is no less a message

than that of the writer whose words march along with

the slow measured tread of plodding men.

One thing is sure, you can't deal with poetry as you

deal with prose.

Allegories must be dealt with as such.

Parables must be recognized as an earthly story with

a heavenly meaning ….

It is not always permissible to make the details of

the parable the basis for certain deductions.

The parable contains an eternal truth, but we must be

careful to remember that the framework of the parable

is only the vehicle through which the truth is

revealed …

else we shall become like the horticulturist who pays

more attention to his flowerpots than the flowers that

grow in them.

(d) In dealing with the logical context, you have to

remember that the writing was produced by a thoughtful

mind ….

[I]t was not an occidental mind, for the author was not

thinking as you and I think.[141]

He had a purpose in writing …

    and he had a way of expressing that purpose that
may be strange to us.
Always in dealing with the Scripture, we must bear in
mind that the logical processes are those of the Oriental.[142]
If you take a small passage by itself, it may seem to
have various meanings …
but its true meaning can never be discovered unless
the passage be considered in the light of the logical
train of thought in the entire writing ….
The writing as a whole—the book
                  or the epistle will reveal a logical
train of thought—an argument—presented in an
oriental way.

You cannot read the book of Kings as you read Ernie Pyle.[143]
See the authors of Scripture as ancient Orientals …
each of whom was different.
The fact that their writings are gathered together
in the canon does not mean that they thought the
same way …
    or followed the same technique in delivering
their message.
(e) No psychological problem is more intriguing than
that of determining what effect the author sought
to create.
He was seeking to make a certain impression upon
the minds of other individuals.
I suggest to you that the book of Revelation is

a good illustration of the sort of psychological

program that faces him who would interpret the Scripture.

I need not tell you how much eisegesis[144] has been

resorted to in dealing with this book of mystery.

You are as familiar as I am with the weird and

wonderful things that so-called Bible students

have dragged out of the apocalypse.

I do not understand the book, and I am frank enough

to admit it.

But this much I do know—it was not written as

a time-table or schedule of the ambitions of Japan

in the Far East …

or to be a blue print of Russia's relation to

Europe after the war.

It was not intended to present detailed information

as to the unfolding of history …

    the rise and fall of nations …

the political intrigues of our time …

or the identity of various world leaders.

Reconstruct the original context, gentlemen.

What was the historical situation that brought

it forth?

The young Christian church some sixty or seventy years

old, had undergone two major persecutions—the

first under Nero[145]

    and the second under Domitian …[146]

with the result that Christianity had become a sort

of under-ground movement.

They had signs and pass-words by which believers made

themselves known to each other.

They met for worship and to observe the Sacrament of

the Lord's Supper in caves and dungeons

            in grottoes and out of the way places

with guards posted to give the alarm at the approach

of Roman soldiers.

They were spied upon and betrayed, for it was a

hazardous thing in those days to be a disciple of "The Way."

A shepherd in the market place would idly trace in

the dust a large "L" …

and the stranger to whom he was speaking, if he were

a Christian, would join to it another capital "L" so

that the cross would be drawn in the sand …

and then hastily rubbed out with the sandaled foot

before others eyes could see …

or it might be the shape of a fish.

It was a hazardous—a dangerous life to be learning

more about Jesus, and to be living in the hope of

His coming.

The author—John—is writing from exile.

He is incarcerated in the Isle of Patmos.[147]

For various reasons, he dare not return to the mainland

or be seen in company with his fellow Christians, lest

he bring new persecutions upon them and subject the

Church to graver danger.

Some Christians not so firmly grounded in the faith

have recanted and fallen away.

New persecutions are threatened.

    The Church faces a crisis.

They who have already suffered much may be called
upon to suffer more ….
And so the apocalypse is written to steady the
faltering
    to encourage the brave
        and to rally the undecided.
It is aimed at the up-building of the highest
kind of morale—the morale that is faithful
unto death.
Very frankly it proclaims the highest rewards to the
Christians who suffer martyrdom for Jesus' sake …
it assures the first readers that the Lord Jesus Christ
is not indifferent to all that they suffer for His sake …
It triumphantly proclaims the ultimate victory of
Christ and His church over the organized forces
of evil …
It predicts dire doom for the empire that sought
with persecution to stamp out what it regarded
as heresy and treason.
Roman swords—already blunted with slaughter—
no longer fitted their sheaths …
Every Christian was carefully watched.
There, gentlemen, is your historical situation.
How, then, is the author to convey his message to the
persecuted?
The same problem today faces the editor of an
underground newspaper in a Nazi-occupied country[148]
but with this difference …
John, himself an Oriental, is writing to Orientals.[149]

He has a vehicle that would not be natural to
a Norwegian or a Frenchman.
He must write so as to be clearly understood …
and yet in such a way as to be unintelligible to
the Romans …
and so he writes in imagery ….
Babylon is Rome …
     the beast is the emperor ….
The great messages of the apocalypse—eternally
true—are to be fitted into the historical
framework of the present day.
Only the original context can reveal the true message
which, however, is always applicable because the
principle is eternal.
But violence is done to the principles of interpretation
when so-called Bible students peruse the pages of
Revelation for some clue as to Stalin's[150] intentions,
or the solution to the enigma that walks like a bear
                    and talks like a man.
The original context, you will agree, is a complicated
thing and sometimes it is impossible to reconstruct
every element in it because some data may be missing.
Therefore, we must resort to theories.
It is not surprising, then, that there should be at
times different interpretations of the same passage.
The theory which the good interpreter will accept
must be in harmony with such elements of the original
context as are discoverable and verifiable.
It is possible to be in a position to discard many

current interpretations as manifestly out of harmony
with the context …
and to be fairly sure that certain other interpretation
is correct according to present information.
Where we are forced to accept a theory, let us remember
that it is always tentative, for we never know when
something will be discovered by an archeologist
                        or an historian
            or a collector of manuscripts
that will throw new light upon any given situation.
Age and experience come to teach us not to become
too dogmatic.
It was when we were in high school or freshmen in
college that we were most sure about things.
Never afterwards have we the same measure of
certainty.
Since graduating from seminary, I have never been
able to achieve the same assurance and confidence
that was mine while a seminary student.[151]
You will find that you can't spin your finely
woven philosophies and expect them to endure
forever ….
They are gossamer things—fragile like spiders'
webs ….
Just when you think you have a formula to fit all
the facts of life, something unexpected and
unpredictable happens, and your logic begins to
look ridiculous ….
Just when you have reached certain conclusions

and arrived at certain estimates of truth …
then life suddenly thrusts something before you
and says:

> All that you say may be true, but this is also
> true.
> The point you make is well taken, nevertheless,
> there is this to be considered.

You will find that in life there is always this
"nevertheless."
The second basic principle of interpretation is
that Scripture must be interpreted by Scripture.

When an interpretation has been arrived at, it
must be checked not only against the background
of the original context …
but also with the general teachings of Scriptures,
the writing as a whole, and the times in which it was written.
Although it must be remembered that in the Old
Testament there is faithfully recorded man's
growing understanding of God …
It is nevertheless true that there is a consistency
about the whole Word of God.
For example, Christ's statement, "I came not to
send peace but a sword"[152] can under no circumstances
be interpreted as advocating armed force in the
establishment of Christ's kingdom …
because that would be absolutely contradictory to the
spirit of Christ and to His teaching as to the methods
by which His kingdom is to be established.

The context clearly reveals that the meaning here
has to do with the divisions that are bound to occur
in families
    and in human relations,
out of loyalty to Christ and His principles.
The reference at the close of Mark's gospel to the
power that was to be given to the first missionaries
whereby "they shall take up serpents;"[153] is not to be
lifted out of its context either literary
                  logical
        and psychological
to mean that we reveal ourselves to have that same
power by handling snakes with impunity.
There have been many snake bites and some deaths from
snake poison as painful object lessons in the folly
of misinterpretations …
the reason being that to impose such a meaning to those
words is to violate not only the whole testimony of
Scripture, but also the intelligence with which God
has equipped us.
A third basic principle of interpretation is that a
particular piece of sacred writing may have two
meanings …
First, the meaning that the original writer wanted the
original reader to get …
and second, the meaning of the writing for ourselves.
I am not trying to suggest that all Scripture has a
double meaning …
but the application of Scripture to our day lies in
the eternal principles it contains, not in the

literal situation that drew it forth.

It is not always easy to see this distinction.

In fact, there are places where the distinction may not exist.

But here, for example, is a place where it is

easy to see the literal application—that is

the historical application—and the eternal.

In I Corinthians, Paul is writing in answer to a

problem that had arisen in the church at Corinth.

Some of the Christians there, converts from

heathen religions—most of them, perhaps having

formerly been Diana worshippers

    or members of the Magna Mater cult[154]

were conscientiously troubled as to what should

be their attitude with regard to meat that had

been offered to idols.

In the public markets, the carcasses that were

offered for sale had been brought from the temples

where the beasts were slaughtered in ceremonial

religious rites …

and then the carcasses sold for public consumption.

These men and women who knew full well all that

went on in the heathen temples.

The issue was crucial.

Since they had embraced the Christian faith and

acknowledged Christ as Lord, would it be right to

get them to eat meat over which pagan rites had

been spoken …

and which to them symbolized all that they had

formerly believed …

and from which they had turned away.
Now that is a problem that will never trouble
you or me.
No such theological questions confront us at
the meat counter …
and yet you can see that it was a very real
problem for the Christians at Corinth.
Now Paul dealt with it, first by pointing out that
there was nothing harmful in the meat itself …
and that it would make no difference to the soul's
relations to Christ whether the stomach contained meat
slaughtered in a heathen temple …

       or fish

         or fowl

           or anything else.
Nevertheless, he went on, if a man who eats such meat
has a troubled conscience, it were better for him to
refrain …
and even if he himself suffered no compunctions
whatsoever, and yet by eating disturbed the consciences
of his brethren …
it were incumbent upon him as a Christian to refrain
because of the eternal principle of Christian
responsibility …
"Wherefore," says Paul, "if meat make my brother to
offend, I will eat no flesh while the world standeth,
lest I make my brother to offend."
And there is the eternal Christian principle which
has a thousand applications in a thousand different
situations today.

Let us recognize the delicacy and the danger in
extracting the eternal principles from a particular
piece of sacred writing.
We know that the Word of God does not exist in a
vacuum, but is set in the midst of life.
It is to apply to every circumstance and situation.
It is the eternal principle revealed in the Scripture
that makes the Word of God true and timeless,
as long as there shall be men upon the earth …
as long as there is sin in the hearts of men …
and as long as their souls are restless in their
seeking after God.
They would know what man is to believe
concerning God—and what
duty God requires of man.
There is only one Book to tell them.[156]

New York Avenue
Presbyterian Church
Washington, D. C.
Established 1803
H. G. Durston

V.

———

ACTION!

The Setting[157]

As Protestant ministers, we must at the outset make
up our minds that the sermon is an essential part
of the worship of God.

Our preaching must be for us an act of worship and
for the congregation, that which makes God real,
and clearly teaches them the application of the
Gospel in their own lives.

Any message from the pulpit which fails in one or
other of these functions is not truly a sermon as the
New Testament regards it.

When the Reformers in their zeal took a courageous
broom to sweep away all that was obnoxious to them
in the Roman Catholic service,

they put the sermon at that point in the service where
the Host had been elevated by the priest.

"The central place which had been taken by the Mass
was claimed for the reading and preaching of the
Word in a context of prayer."[158]

Thus our sermon was given a place of great

responsibility and spiritual significance.
It might well frighten us, as it frightened the
Apostle Paul, who wrote to his friends at Corinth:
"Thus when I came to you … I did not come …
with any elaborate words or wisdom …
it was in weakness and fear and with great trembling."[159]
So ought we to enter the pulpit.
But we must understand that the sermon must have a
setting ….
And the setting is important, not only for itself
and its content of worship ….
But also as a prelude and preparation for the spoken Word.
A worship service, however beautiful and meaningful,
without the sermon, is not a Protestant church
service ….
and the sermon, without an appropriate setting and
introduction cannot possibly fulfill its function in
the hearts and minds of men and women today.
Notice that in most Protestant churches the pulpit is
central, and even where the chancel is divided, the
pulpit still occupies a place of prominence.
Yet far too many Protestants still refer to the interior
of the church as the "auditorium."
Surely it is more than that.
But it is the place where people come to hear—to hear
the preaching of the Word of God.
I cannot object to the view that the sermon is perhaps
the most important element in the service, …
taking as it does, the major portion of the time

allotted to the service …

but I deplore its being regarded as so important that

all which precedes it should be called "the

preliminaries."[160]

But there is something radically wrong with a worship service

that is referred to by those who participate in it as

"preliminaries."

As they mean it, the singing of the hymns

      the prayers

    the music

  and the liturgy of the service are not,

and never could be "preliminaries."

But there is a sense in which they should be

preliminary—that is, in the sense that the whole

service has been planned as a progression toward an

emotional and spiritual climax in which the sermon is

the hammer blow that drives the nail completely home.

"Some people have only one criterion for evaluating the

public worship of God, and that is the quality of the

sermon."[161]

The sermon is not to be regarded as the all-important

part of the service;

neither is it to be minimized by the modesty of the

preacher himself …

or by the excellence of the music …

  or by the beauty of the ritual.

Dr. Denny, a great Scottish theologian of the

last generation,[162] has stated what is, after all,

the whole purpose of preaching, when he said:

"If the sermon in church is what it ought to be—

if it is not an exhibition of the preacher but

of Jesus—

there should be nothing in it even conceivably

in contrast with worship, but the very reverse.

"What can be more truly described as worship than

hearing the Word of God as it ought to be heard,

hearing it with penitence

               with contrition

                    with faith and self-consecration,

        with vows of new obedience?

"If this is not worship in spirit and in truth, what is?"

The sermon must have an appropriate setting.

One does not preach a sermon during the seventh

inning stretch at a ball game.

It would be difficult to make the grandstand a

pulpit in the last of the seventh, with the bases

loaded, and the home team two runs behind.

Nor would the preacher have much success on the floor

of the stock market during a lull in the morning's trading.

The stage of a roadway theatre is not the best

setting for a sermon between acts.

There have been historical exceptions perhaps,

when great preachers, with a fire in their bones,

stood up in the midst of everyday activity, to make

people aware of the higher sanction.

Paul's sermon on Mars Hill certainly lacked the

overtures of praise and the introduction of

worship.[163]

His voice came suddenly into the disputing of the
philosophers, and he had to speak his word when
challenged.
There are times no doubt, when to every preacher there
comes a compulsion to speak, and speak he must,
regardless of the setting.
Ordinarily, however, you and I are to preach in
Protestant churches,
    on Sundays
         and in a particular setting.
Now this setting is important.
It deserves more attention than it receives from the
average minister.

He cannot evade his responsibility by implying that
the setting is not his province …
    but belongs to the organist
         the director of music
      or to someone else.
It is his responsibility—his concern—since it is
the setting in which his message will either lodge in the
hearts and minds of his hearers …
or be lost in a spiritual or ecclesiastical state in
which nothing is very clear to the expectant worshipper
in the pew.
We have constant allies—silent aids and witnesses
speaking for us, and making it easier to direct the
thoughts of the congregation God-ward.
We have the church building itself.
It has associations.

Clinging to its walls are all sorts of hallowed memories.

The voices of loved ones—"loved long since, and lost

awhile"[164] —seem to whisper to lonely hearts.

There are stained glass windows—perhaps—each with

its own message, interpreted by different persons in

different ways.

There is an organ—with its mighty voice speaking as

only organs can speak to the soul.[165]

There are symbols, the cross itself—and who can look

at the cross … and not see something …

who can look at the cross and not hear the voice of Christ?[166]

All these and many more, are our constant silent

partners in the creation of an atmosphere in which

we would present God.

It might be proper to ask at this point, just

what we mean by "atmosphere."

This is one of the things that is difficult to define.

There is no formula for it—but when you have

achieved it—you'll know.

It is like the old question, asked by every adolescent

youth at some time or other: "How will I know when

I fall in love?"

I used to ask it, didn't you?

You know the answer—the only answer that can be

given.

This is the answer I always received; "Don't worry,

brother, you'll know."[167]

Exactly, precisely — you'll know.

Well, when the atmosphere of your service is right,

you'll know.

"The politicians usually have an audience that is

electric ... like prairie grass waiting for the

spark that starts a forest fire.[168]

"Many of the hearers at a political rally are as

keen, for or against, as the speakers themselves,

and "the audience is as thrilled as" those who address

them.

"So with the actor on the stage.

Theatre-goers enter with a sharp and keen expectancy.

They come prepared to listen and to help the actors

in the make believe into which they willingly enter

for two or three hours.

But for the preacher the problem is somewhat

different.

The same eager, sharp expectancy of the theatre is

all too rare in church.

The strong partisan interest that surges through

the audience at a political rally is absent for the

most part.

The preacher, however, has other resources.

He has the promise of the Risen Christ:

    "Wheresoever two or three are gathered together

    in My name, there am I in the midst of them ...."[169]

And the words of the Great Commission:

    "Go ye into all the world, and lo! I am with

    you always, even to the end of the world."[170]

Christ has promised to be present through the Holy Spirit,

It is quite true, and we should never try to evade it,
that our people may meet God anywhere ....
But let us persuade them that they meet Him in a unique
sense among the assembly of Christians.
The Lord is in His church!
gloriously there ... graciously there!

We can "use the whole service for atmosphere,
for creating a receptive and expectant spirit among the
people so that when we come to our preaching, our sermon
may be the natural climax of worship."[171]
The atmosphere is that feeling of spiritual presences,
that glow of the heart
    that confirmation to the soul of the reality of
what it worships ....
That sense of God's nearness, and charges the very
    air, and makes us aware, however we vary in our
spiritual sensitivities, that "truly the Lord is in
this place."[172]
When our people can leave the church with misty eyes,
quiet with the hush of true worship in their hearts,
or when their eyes shine and are eloquent while their
tongues are mute, ...
when they simply clasp your hand and walk away without
speaking ...
then, gentlemen, you have had atmosphere.
In so far as we ourselves can help create this
atmosphere, we should pray for it and plan for it with
every assurance that we can obtain it.

For the promises of God will be as valid next Sunday as
they were last Sunday.

Early in the week—and the earlier the better—
there ought to be a conference between the minister
                         the organist[173]
                    the choir director or director of Music,[174]
whatever he or she may be called.[175]
There is no reason why the ministry and the
musicians should remain in a state of armed
neutrality with regard to each other's work.[176]
There must be a sense of team-work—a partnership:
for each contributes to the effect the others
seek to create.
There is no excuse—nor is there any need for jealousy.
Whatever the music adds to the service and it can
add tremendously, is a help to the preacher.
Every part of the service, should be prayerfully and
carefully arranged so as to co-ordinate the entire
service.
Organ preludes and postludes
                 Interludes and voluntaries should be
consistent with the effect desired.
The hymns should be carefully selected with an eye
to the text as well as the music.
Let no preacher be reluctant to trust his director
of music as to the appropriateness of the hymn tune,
or the type of hymn under consideration.
The director of music will, in most cases, know
better than the preacher, and each ought to recognize

the qualifications of the other in his particular field.

The anthems should likewise be selected with the
same objective in mind so that every part of the
service contributes its own part to the total effect
of the service.

With regard to the hymns, there is here a great
opportunity for training in worship.

You will remember that one of Martin Luther's theses
was his demand that the congregation be given the
right and the privilege of joining in the praise
of God.

"Let all the people praise Him" was an injunction
that had been almost completely ignored until Martin
Luther's time, and sadly enough, has been ignored ever
since in many Protestant churches.

In the last three or four decades, it has become
established custom to hire a professional quartet to
sing God's praises.[177]

It is a source of amazement to me, coming as I do from
a Covenanting background, to see how few there are in
many congregations, that take part in the singing of
the hymns.

I cannot believe that these silent worshippers are
unable to sing. I know better.

I have seen some of them who are mute and unresponsive
to the great hymns of the church, sing lustily enough
at a men's supper or a luncheon club, some of the
popular songs.

Why then this silence on their part in the church service?

Some people, who make no attempt to join in the
singing, would say that they simply "cannot carry a
tune."
I view this excuse with strong suspicion—but, even
if true, they should still be willing to open the hymn
book and read the words that others sing.
Again, others are timid, afraid of the sound of their
own voices, and anxious to avoid being conspicuous when
people around them are not singing.
While there will always be some who for physical reasons
are unable to participate in the praise of God, there
are many more who simply can't be bothered, because it
takes effort to sing and they are not sufficiently
interested.
In church, if people are not familiar with the tune,
they will, for the most part, make no attempt to learn
it ....
But will remain silent and aggrieved that the preacher
doesn't let them sing the familiar hymns.
The average congregation in America, I have read
somewhere, knows only about fifty of the hymns
in the hymnal
Over and over again the same hymns are used
regardless of the date
                the occasion
                    the sermon
            or the mood of the preacher or his people.
How many hymns does the average hymnal contain?
The Presbyterian hymnal contains over five hundred hymns,

but if the people are to use only fifty …

then my Scottish idea of economy is outraged.[178]

Given a choir that loves to sing, there is no reason

why any congregation cannot be taught new hymns—

until its repertoire is expanded and its enjoyment

of singing becomes an experience in real worship.

By using the mid-week service as a teaching service,

as I believe it should be, the hymns to be used

on Sunday can be practised.

Thus you are assured of a nucleus of the congregation

that will be familiar with them.

There are some great hymns, the classics of the

Christian faith that every congregation ought to

know and to use.

If I dared to list them, I should certainly include

Martin Luther's great hymn,

 "Ein' feste Burg ist unser Gott"[179] …

"When I survey the Wondrous Cross" to the tune *Hamburg* ....[180]

"Jesus Lover of my Soul" to the tunes *Refuge* and *Hollingside* ....[181]

 "Ancient of Days"[182]

  "Rock of Ages"[183]

"How Firm a Foundation"[184]

   "Lead, Kindly Light"[185]

"Where Cross the Crowded Ways of Life"[186]

and that lovely evening hymn "The Day Thou Gavest,

    Lord, Is Ended" ....[187]

One could not omit the "Church's One Foundation" to

the tune Aurelia … [188]

nor the marching song of the church—"Onward

Christian Soldiers."[189]

What better Communion hymn could we have than "O Sacred
Head Now Wounded" to Bach's Passion Chorale?[190]
These are but a few of the great hymns that must be
the joy and inspiration of every group of worshipping
Christians.
But there are newer hymns that, in my judgment, will be
just as great when viewed in the perspective of time.
There is Harry Emerson Fosdick's great hymn: "God of
Grace and God of Glory" to the Welsh tune *Cwm Rhondda* ....[191]
The old Irish tune *Slane* is used as the setting for a
hymn which is sung in unison "Be Thou My Vision" ....[192]
The music of Sibelius conveys a message of trust and
confidence in the hymn "Be Still My Soul" ... to the
tune Finlandia.[193]
These are hymns that I would include in the repertoire
of any Protestant congregation.
Yet I have been amazed to find, again and again, that
I could not use them in some church where I was guest
preacher, because the people didn't know them ...
or worse still—the choir didn't know them.
Since I have been reckless enough to list some hymns that
ought to be sung, may I further commit myself by
suggesting some that ought to be avoided?
Many of our congregations' hymns are not good—as music

as poetry

or theology.

The preacher ought to be able to discriminate between
what is good music and bad—but if he cannot—let him
trust his organist or director of music.

If the people can tap their feet to a hymn tune—it is,
more than likely, one to be avoided . . .
and if it be possible to waltz to the melody it were
better to let the dance bands have it.
There are hymns that express a diseased theology, quite
inconsistent with what we believe today.

One such example is the hymn, fortunately not
appearing in our better hymnals, "I was sinking
deep in sin, far from the peaceful shore; very
deeply stained within, sinking to rise no more."[194]
That were bad enough for anyone to sing, but to
ask little children in Sunday School to sing it,
is without excuse.
There are some other hymns whose words surely cannot
be sung by thoughtful Christians without some mental
reservations.
There is a verse in one of our hymns of consecration,
for example, which issues a challenge to God in
these words:

> "Take my silver and my gold, not a mite would
>   I withhold."[195]

Now that is simply going too far—gentlemen—for
your deacons and trustees are not going to mean
that ....
And as they sing that particular hymn, I think you
will notice that they will keep one hand in their
pockets, firmly grasping their roll of bills, and even their loose change.
I was brought up on the psalms and paraphrases, and
have a prejudice in favor of the Scottish Psalter,

I must admit.
But you should have inherited something of the same
tradition in the collection of Bach chorales,[196] so
that we should know better—you and I—than to
permit our people to sing the cheap tunes
                the unnatural in theology
          and the so-called hymns that are not sung
from the heart or the consecrated mind.
We can have great music in our churches …
and have great congregational singing—than which
there is no greater inspiration for the preacher
nor any surer maker of the atmosphere for preaching.
It requires effort to sing, and the diaphragm must
be used as well as the lungs.[197]

With discipline and determination we can have the
kind of music that stirs the soul, without tickling
the toes or shattering the ear-drums.
Being still on the subject of music and its part in the
creation of atmosphere, let me say something about the
choir.
I shall acknowledge at the outset my own bias and
conviction.
I am completely and irrevocably committed to the chorus
choir in preference to the paid quartette.[198]
It is a false economy to try to save money in the budget
item for music, for there is no better investment than
the engaging of a competent choir director.
We have found also, that there is no more active or
successful means of evangelism than our choirs.

Young people brought into the choirs to sing,

    recruited literally from the streets of Washington,

have been introduced to Christ.[199]

Some of them had had no religious education whatsoever,

we found in Washington, young people with no more

religious background than one would expect to find in

the heart of Africa, or in the interior of Tibet.

There is no excuse for any choir or quartet singing

words that are unintelligible to the congregation.

If you cannot make out the words, then the anthem were

better omitted from the service.

It is a message—and was selected as such—not as a

music exercise.

It is to stir the heart—not to tickle the ear.

We have found that it is helpful to have something in

the service to suit every type of worshipper.

They are not all of the same disposition—with the

same tastes

    or the same degree of musical appreciation.

Therefore, we have some of the old hymns and some

of the new ones.

From the gospel hymns we select one that has the

message of the service, as it is used either as an

offertory hymn or as a preparation for the pastoral

prayer.

Here is an important service the choir can render.

As they sing some well-known and beloved hymn of

prayer or aspiration, the preacher can call the

people to prayer …

and the music and message of the prayer hymn is the

most effective creator of atmosphere that I have

yet found.

It is easier to lead the congregation in prayer

when the mood of prayer has been stimulated by

the soft, worshipful singing of a hymn of aspiration.

The anthems, likewise, can provide the old and

familiar as well as the new.

Dudley Buck belongs to the Gay Nineties of church music ...

let him stay there.[200]

Christiansen[201] and Burleigh[202]

    Noble Cain[203] and Roberton[204]

        Dickinson[205] and Tertius Noble[206]

        Emurian[207] and Sibelius[208]

With the masters - Bach and Handel[209]

        Mozart[210] and Rossini[211]

    Mendelssohn[212] and Stainer[213]

provide enough variety and inspiration to keep any choir busy.

The public prayers are perhaps the most difficult

part of the service ...

to keep them free from a formal frigidity on the one

hand ...

and a informal, chatty sentimentality on the other.

The public prayers must be dignified—for we are not

chatting with God ...

and we must avoid sticky adjectives.

There is no place in the pulpit for cheap

familiarity in language.

You cannot talk to God in the light and casual terms

in which you address your next door neighbor.

God is not to be spoken to as if He were the genial

president of your luncheon club. [214]

Rescue yourself from the slack and sloppy affectation

that ruins true reverence.

"Avoid speaking about Jesus as "dear Jesus"

                  "lovely Lord"

              "Sweet saviour" …

terms which are utterly alien to the robust thought of

the New Testament.

No one wants starched dignity—but we do want

reverence."[215]

Invocations should invoke—not argue or orate.

Let the invocation do what it purports to do.

In the pastoral prayer, the minister has the difficult

task of leading his people in prayer.

He has the high privilege of expressing in words of

his own, their deepest thoughts

             and their highest desires.

How can he effectively do that—unless he knows somehow—

what is in their hearts?

How can he possibly know that unless he is personally

acquainted with their needs?

He may discover much in his pastoral visiting

                in his calls in the hospitals

          and in the homes.

He will learn something of the problems facing his

people if he listens carefully when they talk with him.

His conferences in his study are guides to the tumults

raging in some hearts

and the shivering doubts that crouch in others.

Chiefly, however, I feel the minister will find his

surest guides in his own heart.

We know that we "know not what to pray for as we ought,"[216]

but this we do know:

If we pray for what we, as men, need for ourselves,

what we, as parents, feel constrained to prayer for,

we may be sure that we shall be pouring into the molds

of speech some of the unuttered, inarticulate yearnings

of most of the hearts bowed in prayer with us.

One of the most difficult aspects of public prayer

is the avoidance of repetitions.

It is not easy, when one is leading the congregation

twice each Sunday—week after week—to avoid

using the same phrases and sequences of words …

But avoided it must be, at all costs—else the

people, having learned our phrases from constant

repetition—will be saying them ahead of us.

There is a rightful place in our public prayers

for poetic phrases and imagery, for even in our

prayers, the imagination should have a part.

I have a feeling that no part of the average

Protestant service needs more attention—and

receives less—that the reading of the scriptures.

Let the minister remember that he is reading the

Word of God—not the curb market quotations from

yesterday's newspaper.[217]

Let him practise reading the chosen selection, until

he is sure that he can reveal its meaning by his
inflexion.
If the meaning is not clear to him, he will never
be able to make it clear to his congregation.
Here again, and primarily, the minister must feel
what he reads—not stumble through it as if he were
seeing it for the first time, and had not the
slightest idea as to what it might mean.
This is one part of the service where God is speaking
to the people through His word, and the voice of the
minister.
Nothing should be allowed to interrupt or to
detract from this part of the service.
Quiet and reverent attention are more becoming
at this point of the service than at any other ...
for here God is speaking to us.
It behooves us to be more careful here than during
the prayer even, where we are talking to God.
There is more criticism of our services and our
ministers at this point than any other.
Gentlemen—there is absolutely no excuse for slipshod,
unintelligent reading of the Holy Scriptures.
No greater mistake could be made than to assume that it
is easy to read from the Bible.
It is one of the most difficult part of the service,
and one which the sensible preacher will approach with
preparation and dedication.
The Word of God must be so read that every person
present will have heard it, clearly and distinctly, and

will have understood the meaning of the passage from our
reading of it.

Thus we can interpret by the inflexion and emphasis
with which we read.

For your guidance in the reading of the Scripture, make
sure that you have grasped the meaning of the passage …
and then read it with that meaning in mind.

Possibly two of the most familiar passages in the
New Testament are the 14th chapter of John's Gospel,
and the 6th chapter of the Gospel according to Matthew.
Yet I doubt if any passages in the Bible are more often
misread.

No man can serve two masters: for either he will hate
the one, and love the other; or else he will hold to the one,
and despise the other. Ye cannot serve God and mammon.
Therefore I say unto you, Take no thought for your life,
what ye shall eat, or what ye shall drink; nor yet for your
 body, what ye shall put on. Is not the life more than meat,
and the body than raiment?

Behold the fowls of the air: for they sow not, neither do

they reap, nor gather into barns; yet your heavenly Father feedeth them.
Are ye not much better than they?

Which of you by taking thought can add one cubit unto his stature?

And why take ye thought for raiment?

Consider the lilies of the field, how they grow;

 they toil not, neither do they spin:

And yet I say unto you, that even Solomon in all his glory was not arrayed
like one of these.

Wherefore, if God so clothe the grass of the field, which to-day is, and to-morrow is cast into the oven, shall he not much more clothe you, O ye of little faith?

Therefore take no thought, saying, What shall

we eat? Or, What shall we drink? Or,

Wherewithal shall we be clothed?

(For after all these things do the Gentiles

seek:) for your heavenly Father knoweth that

ye have need of all these things.

But seek ye first the kingdom of God, and

his righteousness: and all these things

shall be added unto you. [218]

Let not your heart be troubled: ye believe

In God, believe also in me.

In my Father's house are many mansions: if it were not so,

 I would have told you. I go to prepare a place for you.

And if I go and prepare a place for you,

I will come again, and receive you unto myself;

that where I am, there ye may be also.

And whither I go ye know, and the way ye know.

Thomas saith unto him, Lord, we know not

whither thou goest; and how can we know the way?

Jesus saith unto him, I am the way, the truth,

And the life: no man cometh unto the Father,

But by me.

If ye had known me, ye should have known my Father

also: and from henceforth ye know him, and have seen him.

Philip saith unto him, Lord, show us the Father,

and it sufficeth us.

Jesus saith unto him, Have I been so long time with you,
and yet hast thou now known me, Philip?
He that hath seen me hath seen the Father;
and how sayest thou then, Show us The Father?
Believest thou not that I am in the Father,
and the Father in me? The words that I speak
unto you I speak not of myself; but the Father
that dwelleth in me, he doeth the works.
Believe me that I am in the Father and the
Father in me; or else believe me for the very
works' sake.
Verily verily, I say unto you, He that
believeth on me, the works that I do shall
he do also; and greater works than these shall
he do; because I go unto my Father.
And whatsoever ye shall ask in my name, that
will I do, that the Father may be glorified
in the son.
If ye shall ask any thing in my name, I will
do it.[219]
I believe that the service should proceed to its
climax in the sermon, so that the benediction is
pronounced on a high plane of spiritual experience
and mood.
You will notice that I assume there will be no closing
hymn.
I feel quite definitely that to use a hymn at the close
of the sermon is to interrupt and to shatter
whatever atmosphere has been created.

It is to inject a new note entirely and to dissipate whatever appeal the service, up until then, might have had.

We find it infinitely to be preferred to send the people out under the spell of a great unified service.

To hear the people say, "I enjoyed the whole service" is worth all the effort and careful planning it takes.

If we can have our worshippers think of the service as a whole, we have succeeded in teaching them what worship is.

If your atmosphere has been properly built up, you will feel as you stand up to preach, that psychologically and emotionally, the people are ready for your message.

In fact, it is possible for the experience of worship to be so real and meaningful that the sermon itself may even seem to be anti-climax.

This will not happen very often, but when it does, praise the Lord—for you will then have had the perfect setting for the sermon.

Peter and Catherine Marshall with their son Peter John in the Presbyterian manse
on Cathedral Avenue in Washington, D.C.

VALEDICTORY REMARKS

FRIDAY, MAY 12, 1944

I congratulate you, gentlemen, on the call that
has come to you to become Preachers of the
Word and upon your willingness to accept it.

I salute you, as reinforcements coming to stand beside us
who are already in the line.

If anything I have said has made you want to be a good
preacher—and to say "guid words for Jesus"—

I shall remember these lovely days on your beautiful
old campus with profound gratitude.
God bless you, every one!

This last phrase he spoke in his native Braid Scots (Broad Scots), "guid" meaning "good." In *A Man Called Peter*, Catherine describes how Peter's mother Janet often "lapsed into the 'braid Scots' of her childhood." Her son retained his passion for Scotland even after becoming a naturalized American citizen in 1938.

As president of the St. Andrews Society of Washington, D.C., to raise funds for British War Relief in April 1941, he inaugurated what is known today as the "Kirkin' o' the Tartan." This service is still held annually at Washington National Cathedral, where Dr. Marshall preached at Evensong only 48 hours before he died on January 25, 1949.

AFTERWORD

HONORING PETER MARSHALL'S LEGACY

Linda LeSourd Lader

Seventy-five years after Dr Marshall's death, visitors still stop by The New York Avenue Presbyterian Church in Washington, D.C. to express gratitude for the many ways Peter and Catherine Marshall's ministries have touched their lives. Often, I was the person on-site who was sought out for such conversations.

Why me? In 1959, I was "grafted in" to the Marshall family at age ten when my father, Leonard LeSourd, married Catherine, Peter's widow. Ever after, through books, magazine articles, the film *A Man Called Peter*, and countless conversations, Peter Marshall has remained a significant presence in our extended family. That family includes Peter and Catherine's son, the Rev. Peter John Marshall (1940-2010), his wife, Edith Wallis Marshall (1942-2016) and their children, Mary, Peter, and David, and my brothers, Chester and Jeff LeSourd, our spouses and children, and many others connected in spirit.

For more than two decades, until her death in 1983, Catherine chronicled the challenges, joys, and life-lessons of our combined family in her books and articles. And in her writing, she often described the rocky relationship she and I had as stepmother and stepdaughter. Happily, after—and in part because of—my marriage to Philip Lader, Catherine and I became quite close. Indeed, Phil reminded her of Peter Marshall.

In 2008, with a freshly earned degree from Yale Divinity School and as a candidate for ordination in the Presbyterian Church (PCUSA), I was put in touch with the beloved former pastor of friends in Baltimore. In what seemed to me to be a heaven-ordained serendipity, their friend, the Reverend Dr. Roger Gench, was Senior Pastor at, yes—The New York Avenue Presbyterian Church.

At our first meeting, unaware of my family background, Roger began to tell me about New York Avenue's history and Peter Marshall until, awkwardly, I interrupted to assure him that this was unnecessary. Thus began my warm pastoral collaboration with Roger at The New York Avenue Presbyterian Church lasting from 2008 to 2017.

At times, I imagined Catherine laughing—even rolling her eyes—at the irony that I, of all our family members, served as an ordained Presbyterian minister at "Peter Marshall's church." I like to think that, because of the family connection, my mere presence at the church was meaningful to those drawn by Peter Marshall's ministry.

In his sermons, Dr. Marshall—ahead of his times as he often was—expressed concern for the racial and economic inequities he witnessed in the nation's capital in the 1940s. He personally reached out to disaffected youth, played ball with them, and encouraged them in school. The New York Avenue Presbyterian Church of today carries on dynamic work with the homeless, in racial reconciliation, tutoring young people, and in myriad ministries to those in need.

Because of his premature death in 1949, few recordings exist of Peter Marshall's sermons. They are mostly known through the printed word. Dr. Marshall's published sermons have a distinctive layout, as they follow Peter's own style, with uneven line lengths and "stairstep" indentations. (I confess to having adopted this style for my own sermon manuscripts, although I could never emulate Dr. Marshall's dramatic, evocative style of preaching.)

The New York Avenue Presbyterian Church continues to be known for powerful preachers, each with his or her own style. Though Dr. Marshall's Zimmerman lectures may not have been known to them, preachers at The New York Avenue Presbyterian Church have carried on Dr. Marshall's legacy, often embodying the messages of these Zimmerman lectures.

Energetic, compelling preachers are more commonplace in our day than in Peter's, and most would benefit from the wisdom dispensed by Peter Marshall on these pages. The pitfalls of preaching he warned against indeed loom even larger now, eighty years after these lectures were delivered. Today we are inundated with all manner of media-savvy preachers—some with dubious credentials or theology—on television, YouTube, and social media.

Research historian Margaret Shannon has carefully annotated these lectures, while preserving Dr. Marshall's original phrasing and the integrity of his message. I encourage modern readers not to stumble over his use of male pronouns in reference to people, both male and female, as was customary in Dr. Marshall's time.

Though known to the family, the full lectures have not been published until now. As Margaret Shannon notes in her Editorial Method, Catherine's daughter-in-law Edith Wallis Marshall focused her significant gifts and energy in the last months of her life toward getting these lectures ready for publication. Catherine adored Edith, describing her as the daughter God gave her, and Edith was a wise and cherished older sister to me, as well as our worthy, effervescent family matriarch for more than three decades after Catherine's death.

Edith began working on these Zimmerman Lectures after she was diagnosed with pancreatic cancer in 2015. To her, this project was a gift from God, giving her new purpose as she battled her illness and continued to grieve the unexpected death of her oldest child Mary Elizabeth Marshall at age 43.

> "As I have delved more deeply into the life of Peter Marshall, my father-in-law, I just love the man," Edith enthused. It is the story of an immigrant boy, who began with nothing, but God used him for his glory. He was not a scholar, but a young man who believed that God had his hand on him, God had 'tapped him on the shoulder,' providentially led him to America to train for the ministry, and to become an influential national figure in Washington among Congressmen and the nation as a whole through his life story."

Only weeks before Edith's death in August 2016, the extended Marshall-LeSourd-Lader family gathered at The New York Avenue Presbyterian Church in Washington, D.C. to honor Peter and Catherine Marshall's legacies.

That afternoon, we drove to Annapolis to the United States Naval Academy Chapel to hear Peter Jonathan Marshall read "Rendezvous in Samarra," the sermon his grandfather preached on the morning of December 7, 1941, a date that President Franklin Delano Roosevelt said would "live in infamy."

Midshipmen give thanks for the end of war with Japan on August 14, 1945,
in the U.S. Naval Academy Chapel where Dr. Marshall preached
on the morning of December 7, 1941
—"a date which will live in infamy."

BIOGRAPHICAL SKETCHES

OF PRINCIPAL AUTHORITIES AND SOURCES

The following biographical sketches are adapted from those included in *The Homiletical Theory of Peter Marshall: A Critical Analysis of the Zimmerman Lectures on Effective Preaching*, the master's thesis of Ronald Dean Price (Abilene Christian College, 1971).

JAMES BLACK (1879-1949) At the time of Dr. Marshall's Zimmerman Lectures, Black was minister of St. Georges West, Church of Scotland, Edinburgh. *The Mystery of Preaching* includes the Warrack Lectures on preaching, delivered in the spring of 1923 to the United Free Church Colleges at Edinburgh, Glasgow, and Aberdeen and two chapters added for the James Sprunt Foundation Lectures at Union Theological Seminary in Richmond, Virginia.

PHILLIPS BROOKS (1835-1893) served for twenty-two years as minister of Trinity Church, Boston. Elected Bishop of Massachusetts in 1891, he died less than two years later. Brooks' *Eight Lectures on Preaching*, first delivered at Yale, were published in 1877.

WILLIAM ADAMS BROWN (1865-1938), son of John Crosby Brown, a founder of Union Theological Seminary, earned three degrees from Yale. After graduating from Union Theological Seminary in 1890, he studied with German theologian Adolph Harnack in Berlin. Named Roosevelt Chair of Systematic Theology in 1898 and Research Professor of Applied Theology in 1930, he briefly served as acting president of Yale University.

GEORGE ARTHUR BUTTRICK (1892-1980), born in England, was the pastor of Madison Avenue Presbyterian Church in New York. His Lyman Beecher Lectures for 1930-1931 were published as *Jesus Came Preaching: Christian Preaching in the New Age*. In 1955, he was named professor of

Christian Morals at Harvard and served as president of the Federal Council of Churches in America.

FRANK CAIRNS (1864-1938), a Scottish Congregational minister, delivered the 1924 Warrack Lectures on Preaching, published as *The Prophet of the Heart* (1935), to students of Church of Scotland colleges in Aberdeen and Glasglow.

RALPH WASHINGTON SOCKMAN (1889-1970) was senior pastor of Christ Church Methodist in New York City from 1916 to 1961 and featured speaker on the National Radio Pulpit (NBC) from 1928 to 1962. His 1941 Lyman Beecher Lectures at Yale were published as *The Highway of God;* his Emory University lectures appear in *Recoveries in Religion* (1938). He was appointed associate professor of practical theology, Union Theological Seminary, New York, 1950.

———

BIBLIOGRAPHY

Archives and Libraries

Archives, Agnes Scott College, Papers of Catherine Marshall

Archives, Lutheran Theological Seminary at Gettysburg, Minutes of the Faculty, January 26 and January 31, 1944.

Manuscript Division, Library of Congress, Peter and Catherine Marshall Papers, 1927-1964 MSS31468

Special Collections, University of Iowa, Papers of A. Craig Baird

Theses and Dissertations

Adams, Elizabeth Helen. "An Analysis of Style in Representative Sermons of *Dr. Peter Marshall.*" Master's thesis, University of Michigan, 1953.

Bell, Terry. "A Rhetorical Analysis of the Presentation of the Theology of Dr. Peter Marshall." PhD. diss., Abilene Christian University, 1979.

Berg, William J. "Pictorial Preaching: A Personal Attempt to Apply the Narrative Style of Peter Marshall to Today's Preaching." PhD. diss., Wartburg Theological Seminary, 1985.

Dalstrom, Harl Adams. "Kenneth Wherry." PhD. diss., University of Nebraska-Lincoln, 1965.

Enfield, James R. "The Preaching and Sermons of Peter Marshall." Master's thesis, Baylor University, 1961.

Flory, Elizabeth Bowman. "A Study of the Ethical Proof of Peter Marshall." PhD. diss., Florida State University, 1955.

Hussey, Paul J. "Imagination in the Preaching of Peter Marshall." PhD. diss., New Orleans Baptist Theological Seminary, 2008.

Hyde, Gordon Mahlon. "Rhetorical Study of the Preaching of the Reverend Peter Marshall." Master's thesis, Michigan State University, 1961.

Hyde, Gordon Mahlon. "A Case Study Approach to the Rhetorical Analysis of the Washington Preaching of Dr. Marshall." PhD. diss., Michigan State University, 1964.

Laux, John A. "A Literary Analysis of Selected Peter Marshall Sermons." PhD. diss., Concordia Theological Seminary, 1985.

McAlister, Virginia. "A Rhetorical Analysis of Style in Selected Recorded Sermons of Dr. Peter Marshall." PhD. diss., Kansas State College of Pittsburg, 1964.

McDow, Malcolm. "A Study of the Preaching of Peter Marshall." Master's thesis, New Orleans Baptist Theological Seminary, 1965.

Morgan, Jimmie Morton. "A Rhetorical Analysis of the Senatorial Prayers of Peter Marshall." Master's thesis, University of Alabama, 1956.

T. Farrar Patterson. "Analysis of Selected Gettysburg Lectures." Master's thesis, Texas Christian University, 1968.

Price, Ronald Dean. "The Homilectical Theory of Peter Marshall: A Critical Analysis of the Zimmerman Lectures on Effective Preaching." PhD. diss., Abilene University, 1971.

Ragland, Larry Clarke. "A Thematic Analysis of the Published Sermons of Peter Marshall." Master's thesis, Texas Christian University, 1966.

Romeis, David. "The Prayers of Peter Marshall in the U.S. Senate." Master's thesis, Stanford University, 1967.

Stromer, Marvin Edward. "The Making of a Political Leader: Kenneth S. Wherry and the United States Senate." PhD. diss., University of Nebraska - Lincoln, 1966. http://digitalcommons.unl.edu/dissertations/AAI6613121

BOOKS

Baxter, Richard. "Love Breathing Thanks and Praise," Pt. 2, St. 29. in Black, James. *The Mystery of Preaching*. New York: Fleming H. Revell Co. 1924.

Brooks, Phillips. *The Joy of Preaching*. London: H. R. Allenson, 1895.

Buttrick, George A. *Jesus Came Preaching: Christian Preaching in the New Age,* New York: Charles Scribner's Sons, The Lyman Beecher Lectures for 1930-31.

Cairns, Frank. *The Prophet of the Heart.* New York: Harper and Brothers, 1935.

Daugherty, George M. *I've Seen the Day.* Grand Rapids, Mich.: William B. Eerdmans Publishing Company, 1984.

Denny, James. *The Way Everlasting: Sermons by James Denny.* London: Hodder and Stoughton, 1911.

Ellinwood, Leonard W. *The History of American Church Music.* New York: Morehouse-Gorham Company, 1953.

Elson, Edward L. R. *Wide Was His Parish: An Autobiography.* Tyndale House, 1986.

Erdman, Irwin. *Adam, The Baby, and the Man from Mars.* Cambridge: Houghton Mifflin Co., 1929.

Link, Henry Charles. *The Return to Religion.* New York: The MacMillan Co., 1936.

Lutkin, Peter. *Music in the Church.* Milwaukee: The Young Churchman Co., 1910.

Marshall, Catherine. *A Man Called Peter.* New York: McGraw-Hill Book Co., 1951.

_______________. *To Live Again.* New York: Fleming H. Revell Company, 1957.

_______________. *Mr. Jones, Meet the Master,* 5th ed. New York: Fleming H. Revell Co., 1950.

_______________. *The Prayers of Peter Marshall,* ed. Catherine Marshall. New York: McGraw-Hill, 1952.

Montague, Charles Edward. *Rough Justice.* London: Chatto and Winters, 1928.

Newton, Joseph Fort. *The New Preaching: A Little Book about a Great Art.* Nashville, Tenn.: Cokesbury, 1930.

O'Shaughnessy, Arthur William, ed. *Poems of Arthur O'Shaughnessy*, William Alexander Percy. New Haven: Yale University Press, 1923.

Presbyterian Church in the U.S.A. The Constitution of the Presbyterian Church of the United States containing the Confession of Faith. Richmond, Va.: Presbyterian Committee on Publication, 1910.

Quayle, William A. *The Pastor-Preacher*. Cincinnati: Jennings and Graham, 1910.

Selden, John, Edward Arber, ed. *Table-Talk*. London: A Murray and Son, 1868.

Shakespeare, William. *Shakespeare's Works*, ed. C. H. Herford. New York: MacMillan Co., 1902.

Shaw, George Bernard. *Saint Joan: A Chronicle Play in Six Scenes and an Epilogue*. New York: Brentano's, 1924.

Sheen, Fulton J. *The Eternal Galilean*. New York: D. Appleton-Century Company, Inc, 1934.

Sockman, Ralph. *The Highway of God*. New York: The Macmillan Co., 1943. The Lyman Beecher Lectures for 1941 at Yale University.

________________. *Recoveries in Religion*. Nashville: Tenn.: Cokesbury Press, 1938.

Thonssen, Lester and A. Craig Baird. *Speech Criticism*. New York: The Ronald Press Company, 1948.

Wentz, Abdel Ross. *Gettysburg Lutheran Theological Seminary History*, Vol. I. Harrisburg, Penn.: The Evangelical Press, 1964.

PERIODICALS

Hyde, Gordon Mahlon. "A Case Study Approach to the Rhetorical Analysis of the Washington Preaching of Dr. Peter Marshall." *Speech Monographs*, 31 (August 1964), 248.

McAlister, Virginia Clemens, and Mary M. Roberts. "Peter Marshall's Sermon Approach—Innovative or Traditional?" *Southern Speech Journal*, XXXV (Summer, 1970), 315-323.

Marshall, Catherine. "Sermon-Writing the Hard Way." *Pulpit Book Club Bulletin* (Dec.,1949).

Marshall, Peter. "The Setting of the Sermon." *Religion in Life* 14, no. 2 (Spring, 1945), 195-204.

Lutheran Theological Seminary. "Gettysburg Seminary Week," in *Gettysburg Seminary Bulletin*, 24, no. 2 (May 1944), 3-4.

Lutheran Theological Seminary. "The Power of Preaching," *Gettysburg Seminary Bulletin*, 24, no. 3 (Aug. 1944), 8-9.

Lutheran Theological Seminary. *Catalogue Number Bulletin*, 24, no. 1 (Feb., 1944), 42-43.

Prussing, Stephen H. "Enter the Kingdom Singing: The Story of The New York Avenue Presbyterian Church Choir," *The Choral Journal* 10, no. 4 (Jan.1970), 18-20. Stable URL: http://www.jstor.org/stable/23543250

NEWSPAPERS

The Washington *Evening Star*

The *Washington Post*

The Nebraska State *Journal and Star*

The *Lincoln Star*

Gettysburg Times

New York *World*

GOVERNMENT DOCUMENTS

Congressional Record. 76 Cong., 3d sess., House November 11, 1940. House, p. 13613, Vol. 86, Appendix p. 6574-6575.

"Prayers offered by the Chaplain, the Rev. Peter Marshall, D.D. / at the opening of the daily sessions of the Senate during the Eightieth and Eighty-first Congress 1947-1949. Senate Doc 80-170. Washington: Government Printing Office, 1947

ACKNOWLEDGEMENTS

Edith Wallis Marshall Roberts (1942-2016), daughter-in-law of Peter and Catherine Marshall and wife of their son, Peter John Marshall. Edith first envisioned publication of these lectures and worked tirelessly on the project. Before her untimely death in 2016, she extracted a promise from the Marshall – LeSourd family members to see this joint venture to fruition. We do so now, in thanksgiving for Edith's life and the faith and strength she radiated through times of joy and of sorrow: the loss of three children, including her daughter Mary Elizabeth at the age of 43 in 2012.

- *To the Marshall family* – Dr. Peter Marshall (1902-1949), his wife Catherine Marshall LeSourd (1914-1983) son Peter John Marshall (1940-2010), daughter-in-law Edith Marshall (1942-2016), granddaughter Mary Elizabeth Marshall (1969-2012), and to their living grandsons David Christopher Marshall and Peter Jonathan Marshall, whose Preface perfectly incapsulates his mother's vision for this book.

- *To the LeSourd family* – Linda LeSourd Lader and Hon. Philip Lader; Chester and Susan LeSourd; Jeff and Nancy LeSourd – for their support and encouragement throughout the work of bringing these timely lectures to generations of new or established ministers.

- *To Nancy Oliver LeSourd, Esq.*, intellectual property attorney at Gammon & Grange, P.C. and publications manager and steward of the Catherine Marshall and Dr. Peter Marshall works for the Marshall-LeSourd family.

This volume would not have been possible without the research, bibliographical annotations, and editorial methodology of Margaret Shannon, the Marshall-LeSourd family archivist and historian for five decades. She first saw the movie "A Man Called Peter" in 1955 at the American Embassy in Oslo, Norway.

For kindnesses large and small, we are grateful to Virginia Theological Seminary Professor *Emerita* Dr. Mitzi Budde, who provided invaluable research as did John O'Brien, archivist of The New York Avenue Presbyterian Church. Thanks as well to Larry Taylor, of Larry Taylor Design, Ltd. for cover and interior design.

For his assistance to Edith Marshall Roberts in locating the original Zimmerman lecture manuscripts in the Library of Congress, we thank the Rev. Dr. Mark Bumpus, longtime pastor of the First Baptist Church in San Angelo, Texas.

EDITORIAL NOTES

Abbreviations

AMCP - *A Man Called Peter*

CM - Catherine Marshall LeSourd

DPM - Dr. Peter Marshall

NYAPC - The New York Avenue Presbyterian Church

Format

The Rev. Peter Marshall regularly preached from a prepared text. His Zimmerman Lectures followed the same format. He drafted his lectures, addresses, sermons, even radio broadcasts on his own Royal #10 typewriter, with some letters out of alignment. He typed, single-spaced, on an 8.5" x 11" sheet of white paper, often crossing out words or phrases, as he went. Catherine Marshall described his writing process in *AMCP*.

> The preacher's workshop was his office at the church. This was a tiny room on the second floor whose windows looked out on New York Avenue, right in the heart of downtown Washington. Books lined two sides of the room almost to the ceiling …. If Peter raised the windows, he had to concentrate above the roar of the traffic, the rumble of ancient streetcars, the ear-splitting staccato of inevitable pneumatic drills. If he closed the windows, he suffered with the heat—which he was certain had been sent as a Scotsman's personal cross.

> He worked under great pressure. Over and over the telephone interrupted his determined effort to meet his deadline. He would

type a page, call to his secretary from the top of the stairs, and the sheet would go fluttering into the downstairs hall. Then, while he worked on page two, she would be typing page one into the unusual form of the complete manuscript from which he always preached.

As a young minister, Peter had been intrigued by the sermon manuscripts of Dr. Trevor Mordecai of Birmingham, Alabama, a Welshman whose preaching he had much admired. Dr. Mordecai had devised a way of typing his sermons that had assisted him in delivery. Peter had found the idea useful and had adapted it to suit his own needs ....

The device had two chief characteristics: all lists or series of nouns, adjectives, phrases, or even descriptive clauses were typed in stair-step fashion; and every new sentence was typed flush with the left-hand margin rather than being indented.

Annotation

The five Zimmerman Lectures in this volume have been meticulously annotated with contextual and textual endnotes to provide details about persons or events that were common knowledge to his 1944 and 1948 audiences, such as passing references to poems, hymns, and World War II-era personalities.

For example, in Lecture V, he said "Clinging to [the church's] walls are all sorts of hallowed memories. The voices of loved ones — 'loved long since and lost awhile' — seem to whisper to lonely hearts." That he spoke these words without reference to the source indicates he knew how familiar they would be to his hearers. For today's readers, this and similar passing references have been fully identified.

Editorial Style

The tangible, fixed texts from which Dr. Peter Marshall (DPM) preached and spoke reflect inconsistent decisions made by his typists, rather than DPM, on the precise formatting of the text. For example, ellipses vary from three to five to seven. The editors have adhered to the *Chicago Manual of Style*, 17th edition (CMS), and *Merriam-Webster's Collegiate Dictionary*, 11th edition, with exceptions not inconsistent with documentary editing standards. We have:

- Retained his British spellings of words (e.g., theatre, humour).

- Retained his use of double consonants (e.g., worshipping).

- Conformed his initial caps style of God pronouns.

- Conformed ellipses to CMS.

- Corrected silently misspelled proper names (e.g., Niemöller).

- Corrected silently clear typographical errors (e.g., sould/soul).

- Added punctuation silently as necessary for comprehension.

- Replaced typed double hyphens with 2-em dashes.

- Retained DPM's original quotation marks even when indented.

- Cited all biblical quotations to his King James Bible.

- Cited all material identified as attributable to others.

- Added quotation marks if missing in DPM typescript.

No words in these Lectures have been altered, omitted, or added. They have been transcribed from microfilm copies of his original typescripts, in the Peter and Catherine Marshall papers at the Library of Congress.

THE 1948 LECTURES

The editors determined—from internal evidence in the manuscripts and through newspaper databases—that Dr. Marshall delivered these five Lectures at least twice—first, as the Zimmerman Lectures on Effective Preaching at Gettysburg Theological Seminary in May 1944 and then, in April 1948, as lectures to the Nebraska Clergy Conference in Lincoln.

In the intervening years, much had changed. In May 1944, D-Day was still four weeks away. Four years later, in April 1948, the atomic bomb had been dropped, World War II had ended, the Cold War had begun, and the first presidential campaign since Franklin Roosevelt's death was underway.

In preparation for the 1948 Lectures, DPM edited outdated references on his original manuscript. Thus, "Stalin" replaced "Hitler" and Winston Churchill's "Iron Curtain" superseded the "War in Europe." These were clues that led to discovering where and when he had repeated these Lectures.

Self-borrowing in
Dr. Marshall's Sermons and Lectures

Two iconic eighteenth-century composers—George Frideric Handel and Johann Sebastian Bach—regularly parodied their own works; that is, they reworked and repurposed melodies from other composers as well as their own. Bach's Mass in B Minor, his monumental *summa*, borrows or reworks previously composed material. Juilliard-trained Paul W. Hofreiter, explains:

> During the Baroque period it was standard practice to borrow music from one's own output as well as that of other composers. There were no concerns of copyright infringement. On the contrary, the use of another composer's material arranged or transcribed for other musical purposes was even viewed as eulogistic. For Bach this technique of musical composition was no exception as he arranged the music of other composers for his own purposes on occasion. (For instance, three Vivaldi instrumental concerti Bach arranged for organ.)

Like these master musicians, Peter Marshall has been acknowledged as one of the great preachers of the twentieth century. He, too, borrowed from himself—and others. He kept an index of his sermon illustrations and subjects, which he would "recycle" for new occasions before different audiences. For example, the chemical elements illustration used in Lecture IV also appears in the sermon Dr. Marshall delivered at the U.S. Naval Academy on the morning of December 7, 1941.

Attribution

With the exception of a few radio broadcasts, for all but the last of Dr. Marshall's seventeen years as an ordained minister (May 1931- Jan. 1949), his spoken words were heard only by those physically present in the venue where he spoke—be it a church, a lecture hall, a seminary, or the United States Senate. There were no YouTube channels or smart phones to record and upload within minutes the mesmerizing poetic cadences of his Scots brogue. Witness the long lines of people who waited patiently, even in the rain, to gain a seat in the church or auditorium every time he preached.

As the demand for copies of his sermons grew, NYAPC printed small sermon pamphlets that sold for twenty-five cents. He was clearly aware of the need for full and complete attribution required by publication as opposed to his customary informal credit in oral delivery. A recently discovered letter confirms Dr. Marshall made written requests for permission to publish material he had used in his sermons.

As word of his preaching spread across America, Dr. Marshall turned down repeated requests to publish his sermons for a wider audience, saying they were not good enough. Asked in 1948 by a Presbyterian Church publisher, "when the time might come," DPM indicated that he "wanted to use them a while longer before publication." Several sermons, however, slipped through his firm control. At the request of Rep. Sam Hobbs of Alabama, a NYAPC member, the *Congressional Record* published excerpts from one of Dr. Marshall's most popular sermons, "The Man with the Bowler Hat," which he had preached on September 29, 1940, at NYAPC. DPM declined to allow this sermon to be included in a volume of *Representative American Speeches* compiled annually by A. Craig Baird. "I do not consider it," DPM wrote the University of Iowa professor, "as representative of my preaching since it does not contain elements which I seek in my best efforts." "*Someday*," he added, "perhaps I shall have attained that degree of proficiency for which I am still striving."

Someday.

In the early morning hours of Tuesday, January 25, 1949, Dr. Marshall died after his second massive heart attack in less than three years. Six weeks later, his 34-year-old widow Catherine found herself surrounded by friends helping to read through more than six hundred extant sermon manuscripts to select twelve for a book of Peter's sermons. *Mr. Jones, Meet the Master* became an instant best seller. Its initial print run sold out before publication day in November 1949.

One of its many readers was Leslie Weatherhead (1893-1976), the pastor of London's City Temple and a popular Christian author. He was dismayed to discover in several of Marshall's sermons passages from his own writings that were not properly acknowledged. Catherine, who had recently recovered from the illness that kept her bedridden for three years, and her publisher Fleming H. Revell, had undertaken difficult due diligence in reviewing DPM's library books and sermon manuscripts, which were his "work product." In no sense could they be considered final drafts suitable for publication. Time had simply run out for Peter before his hoped-for "someday."

Accordingly, when the fifth edition of *Mr. Jones, Meet the Master* was published in March 1950, Revell included additional and detailed acknowledgements of indebtedness to material by Weatherhead. Three different sermons replaced three previously published "book sermons" that were deemed too indebted to others. In her introduction to *A Man Called Peter*, her best-selling biography of Peter written two years after his death, Catherine gave a fuller explanation of the attribution process.

> Since Dr. Marshall had no idea that a book of his sermons would ever be published, the sermon manuscripts which he left behind were not completely annotated. Often he gave informal oral credit to others from the pulpit. Such statements were not always incorporated into his manuscripts. Thus, the task of uncovering all sources of indebtedness to others has been a difficult one.
>
> In preparing the present volume I have undertaken the most careful and conscientious research, and in footnotes throughout the book have given proper credit in each instance in which I was able to discover that quoted material had been used. It is possible, however, that I have not been able to identify every single instance of this kind. If, therefore, there should remain any unacknowledged quotation in the sermons or the sermon excerpts in this book, I shall welcome information to that effect and shall be glad to credit such material to the proper source in future editions of this book.

When Catherine Marshall prepared her husband's sermons for inclusion in *Mr. Jones, Meet the Master* in 1949 and in *A Man Called Peter*, neither she nor her publishers—indeed no one—had available today's powerful digital search engines of Google Books, HathiTrust, and software such as iThenticate™ to aid in her search for any uncredited sources. These twenty-first century research and bibliographic tools have enabled the editors of these Lectures to identify more fully and completely the sources to whom credit is rightfully due.

We have undertaken the most rigorous examination of every line, using the most sophisticated technology available in addition to old-fashioned reading, page by page, of hard-copy editions of books upon which Dr. Marshall relied. Yet, we join with Peter and Catherine Marshall "across time and circumstance" to affirm once again that, "should there remain any unacknowledged quotation in the Lectures, we shall welcome information to that effect and give proper credit in future editions."

SOLI DEI GLORIA

Like the music of Bach and Handel, Peter Marshall's sermons have changed countless lives, not only of those who heard him in person but also, in the nearly eighty years since his death, of the millions whose lives have been touched through the Catherine Marshall's biography and the film of *A Man Called Peter*.

As with Bach and Handel, whose musical scores they inscribed *Soli Dei Gloria*, (to the glory of God alone,) Marshall said, "I have determined to give my life to God for Him to use me wherever he wants me."

Each generation discovers anew the irrepressible joy of Bach and Handel.

So too, the enduring legacy of "a man called Peter."

Peter Marshall.

CONTRIBUTORS

Peter Jonathan Marshall, grandson of Peter and Catherine Marshall and son of the late Peter and Edith Wallis Marshall, is founder of Peter Marshall & Company CP in Texas. Peter is a graduate of The McCallie School and Presbyterian College.

Philip Lader, former U.S. Ambassador to the Court of St. James's and member of President Clinton's Cabinet, was Chairman of the global advertising/communications firm, WPP plc, Vice Chairman of RAND Corporation, Senior Advisor to Morgan Stanley, and a director of Lloyds of London and numerous international companies. Educated at Duke, Michigan, Oxford, and Harvard Law School, he served as president of two universities and has been awarded honorary doctorates by fourteen other universities.

Linda LeSourd Lader, the daughter of Leonard LeSourd and stepdaughter of Catherine Marshall, is a graduate of Ohio Wesleyan University and Yale Divinity School and is an ordained Presbyterian minister. Linda, with her husband Philip Lader, founded Renaissance Weekends in 1981, the non-partisan retreats that seek to build bridges between innovative leaders from diverse fields.

Edith Wallis Marshall Roberts (1942-2016), a daughter of medical missionaries, earned her B.A. degree from Trinity College in San Antonio, Tex., and attended Princeton Theological Seminary where she met and, in May 1965, married Peter John Marshall. A social worker in Hyannis, Mass, she held a M.A. from Boston University School of Social Work.

Margaret Shannon, a research historian with a B.A. in history and music from Transylvania University, established Washington Historical Research in 1978 at the urging of her mentor Catherine Marshall for whom she researched the novel, *Julie*. A curator of exhibitions at the Library of Congress, U.S. Holocaust Memorial Museum, and Washington National Cathedral, she is the Cathedral Choral Society's longtime award-winning program annotator. She has collaborated closely for over two decades with Pulitzer Prize-winning presidential historian Jon Meacham.

IMAGE CREDITS

Dr. Peter Marshall at Saint Andrew's Society Gala, Waldorf Astoria, November 20, 1945. Courtesy of Saint Andrew's Society of the State of New York

Edith Wallis Marshall Roberts
Family Archives

Dr. Peter Marshall Scripture in his Handwriting
Peter and Catherine Marshall Papers
Library of Congress Manuscript Division

Dr. Peter Marshall Signature
Family Archives

Peter Jonathan Marshall
Family Archives

Philip J. Lader
Family Archives

Harry S. Truman Inauguration
The Rev. Dr. Peter Marshall, U.S. Senate chaplain and Senator Arthur Vandenberg, president pro tempore, lead Senators onto the platform for the inauguration of Harry S. Truman on January 20, 1949.

Harry S. Truman Library & Museum, Accession Number 64-1-51. Originally published by *The Washington Post*, Arthur Ellis, photographer. Used with Permission.

Catherine Marshall Signature
Family Archives

Class of 1944, Lutheran Theological Seminary
Image courtesy of Seminary Archives, A.R. Wentz Memorial Library, United Lutheran Seminary [ULS.LTSG.007.005.021].

Dr. Peter Marshall in the Pulpit
The New York Avenue Presbyterian Church, Washington, D.C.
Family Archives

Dr. Peter Marshall in Sermon Preparation in his Office.
The New York Presbyterian Church, Washington D.C.
Family Archives

Dr. Peter Marshall, Easter Service, Fort Lincoln Heights,
Washington, D.C., April 5, 1942
Library of Congress, Prints and Photographs Division, Washington, D.C.   FSA/OWI – John Ferrell

Dr. Peter Marshall with his 5" x 7" Sermon Notebook
Family Archives

The New York Avenue Presbyterian Church Bulletin Cover
The New York Avenue Presbyterian Church Archives
Helen Gasch Durston, Artist

Peter and Catherine Marshall with their son Peter John in the Presbyterian manse on Cathedral Avenue, Washington, D.C.
Family Archives

Linda LeSourd Lader
Family Archives

Chapel, United States Naval Academy on August 14, 1945
Midshipmen in the Academy chapel give thanks for the end of the war with Japan, 14 August 1945
Special Collections & Archives, Nimitz Library, USNA

ENDNOTES

1. This introduction, the only currently known extant original typescript associated with these lectures, is in the Peter and Catherine Marshall Papers, Manuscript Division, Library of Congress, Box 32, Folder 2.

2. "The World's Bible," by Annie Johnston Flint (1866-1932)

3. John 15:5

4. Philippians 4:13

5. Mark 3:14

6. Acts 17:6

7. Original: "The church is not a gallery for the better exhibition of eminent Christians, but a school for the education of imperfect ones." J. Edward Close, *Our Church and Her Interests: Being a Souvenir of the Past History and a Survey of the Present and Future Interests of the First Presbyterian Church of Jordan, Onondaga County, New Jersey, 1877.*

8. Ralph Washington Sockman, *Recoveries in Religion* (Nashville, Tenn.: Cokesbury Press, 1938).

9. This is a passing reference to "We fall in a war with Time which knows no armistice," in Lawrence Binyon's poem, "For the Fallen," and incorporated by Winifred Holtby (1898-1935) in her short story, "The Casualty List" (1932), first collected in *Truth is Not Sober* (1934).

10. William Shakespeare, *Merchant of Venice,* Act III/Scene I, Lines 60-70.

11. Sockman, *Recoveries in Religion*, 254, quoted by Theodore Engelder in his review, *Concordia Theological Monthly*, Vol IX, No. 5 (May, 1938), 395.

12. "We are the Music Makers," an ode by the English poet Arthur O'Shaughnessy (1844-1881) published in *Music and Moonlight*, 1874. In DPM's sermon, the poem is erroneously attributed to Otto Rudolph (1869-1937), a German Lutheran theologian.

13. DPM graduated *magna cum laude* from Columbia Theological Seminary on May 20, 1931. In an unusual step, the Seminary faculty agreed to accept his educational work in Scotland as an equivalent to a bachelor of arts degree, See *AMCP*, 33. Here, he revised this text for the 1948 Lincoln Lectures to reflect the passage of seventeen years.

[14] Original: "communication of truth by man to men. It has in it two essential elements, truth and personality. Neither of these can it spare and still be preaching." Phillips Brooks, *Lyman Beecher Lectures at Yale University*, 1877, 5.

[15] Sockman, *Recoveries in Religion*, 269

[16] Original: "Preaching is the art of making a preacher and delivering it? Why no! Preaching is the art of making a sermon and delivering that." Methodist Episcopal Bishop William A. Quayle (1860-1925), *The Pastor-Preacher*, The Methodist Book Concern, New York: Jennings and Graham, 1910, p. 363.

[17] Original: "It might be said here that to become a doctor of humanity is more difficult than to become a doctor of divinity. For the former, one must cultivate all classes and conditions of men, while for the latter he need cultivate only one college president." Sockman, *Recoveries in Religion*, 2.

[18] Sockman, *Recoveries in Religion*, 278, quoting Stephen Leycock (1869-1944) in *Gertrude the Governess, or, Simple Seventeen*.

[19] "We tried to have a few quiet moments together in our bedroom before breakfast. On these mornings when we gave our day into God's hand and asked Him to bless it, we found that for each of us the whole day went more smoothly. There was a reassuring feeling of accomplishment at the end of it. When we omitted this brief prayer time together, things became snarled. We felt that we were battling uphill against terrific odds for meager accomplishment." Catherine Marshall (CM) in *A Man Called Peter* (hereafter *AMCP*), 120: CM may have drafted this for the Lecture and later paraphrased herself in *AMCP*.

[20] Stockman, *Recoveries in Religion*, 160, paraphrasing psychologist Henry C. Link, *The Return to Religion*, (New York: The MacMillan Company, 1936).

[21] John Selden (1584-1654), English jurist in *Table Talk, Being the Discourses of John Selden, Esq., Relating especially to Religion and State*, (London: J. M. Dent and Co., 1689).

[22] Anonymous. Quoted by Eric Hiscock in *Cruising Under Sail*, (London: Oxford University Press, 1950).

[23] James Alexander Bryan, known as Brother Bryan (1863-1941), was pastor of Third Presbyterian Church in Birmingham, Alabama. A strong advocate of civil rights and racial harmony, he attended, but did not graduate from, Princeton Theological Seminary. The statue of Brother Bryan erected in 1934 is one of Birmingham's best-known landmarks. He remained DPM's good friend and co-officiated at his funeral.

[24] Often attributed to Baptist preacher Charles Haddon Spurgeon, these four lines are an apparent paraphrase of the Apostle Paul's defense during his trial before the Roman governor, as recorded in the Book of Acts 24:12: "Yet they did not find me arguing with anyone in the temple."

[25] DPM added "diocese, conference, or convention" for the 1948 Lectures to the Nebraska Clergy Conference.

[26] Matthew 7:14

[27] Presbyterian Installation ... *PCA Book of Church Order* 24-6 (6.)

28 In *The History of Fundamentalism*, Richard R. Smith, Inc., 1931, Steward G. Cole identified the group as the Baptist Bible Union of North America.

29 *The Fundamentalist* (Dec. 15, 1923), 24, quoting a *New York World* editorial.

30 Theologian Hugh Black (1868 –1953). a native of Scotland, was a professor at Union Theological Seminary.

31 Original: 'Dummies, my dear boy,' said Bob Sawyer; 'half the drawers have nothing in 'em, and the other half don't open.' Charles Dickens, *The Pickwick Papers* (1836-1837), Chapter 38.

32 Original: "Devotion is like the candle which Michelangelo used to carry stuck on his forehead in a paste-board cap, and which kept his own shadow from being cast upon his work when he was hewing out his statues." Phillips Brooks, *Heart's-Ease*, (New York: Cupples & Leon Company, 1909).

33 Possible paraphrase of Henry Frank Lott, "Reminiscences of Poets and The Songs" in *The Bombay Miscellany*, J. Higgonbotham, ed. 1862, 128.

34 For the 1948 lectures, DPM revised this number to three.

35 In 1943, race riots broke out in these and other American cities.

36 These lectures were delivered on May 10-13, 1944, one month before the Normandy Invasion in the fifth year of World War II in which Hitler's lawlessness was beyond anything ever known.

37 Original: "The prophet irritates, prods, denounces, stands alone in his demands, insists on applying God's eternal principles of life. He is an ethical teacher, a moral reformer, a dangerous disturber of men's minds. He constantly strikes at sins, vices and lapses and seeks to stir men to holier lives." Kyle Monroe Yates (1895-1975), *Preaching from the Prophets,* (New York: Harper & Brothers, 1942).

38 Ephesians 6:12 English Standard Version (ESV)

39 Hugh Latimer and Nicholas Ridley, bishops of the English Church, were burned at the stake on order of Queen Mary in Oxford on October 16, 1555.

40 Dwight L. Moody (1837-1899), a nineteenth-century American evangelist and publisher, founder of Moody Bible Institute, and the Northfield schools in Massachusetts.

41 Adoniram Judson, Jr. (1788-1850) was an American Congregationalist who became a Baptist missionary serving in Burma for nearly forty years.

42 Eivind Berggrav (1884-1959) was the Lutheran bishop and primate of the Church of Norway who refused to yield to the Nazis, remaining under house arrest during their occupation of Norway from 1940-1945.

43 Pastor Martin Niemöller (1893-1984) was a German theologian and a founder of the German Confessing Church. Although a member of the NSDAP, for his opposition to the Nazis' state control of the churches, Niemöller was imprisoned 12 years in Sachsenhausen and Dachau concentration camps. His friend Dietrich Bonhoeffer (1902-1945) was executed April 8/9, 1945, on Hitler's direct order for participating in the failed assassination attempt on Hitler on July 20, 1944.

44 William Shakespeare, *As You Like It*, Act II, Scene IV

45 Richard Baxter (1615-1691), an English Puritan church leader, poet, hymn-writer, theologian, and controversialist, in *Poetical Fragments*, printed for J. Dunton, 1689, 30.

46 "Pastor's Doctrine Blocks Coast Call," *The Washington Post* (Aug. 31, 1940), regarding the First Presbyterian Church in Seattle.

47 CM quotes from "notes made for a sermon to ministers which Peter called 'The Perils of a Preacher,' regarding 'the dangers of popularity, praise, and flattery, [to which] he had added that of 'designing women.'" *AMCP*, 47.

48 CM quotes this anecdote in *AMCP*, 169: 'I shall not soon forget the indictment I heard in my little boy's prayer one night. 'Thank you, God,' he prayed, 'that you let my daddy stay home this one evening!' Peter John Marshall (1940-2010) was educated at Sidwell Friends in Washington, D.C., and Mount Hermon in Northfield, Mass. He earned his bachelor's degree in history at Yale University (1961), a Master of Divinity from Princeton Theological Seminary (1964), and was ordained in 1965. After pastorates in Connecticut and Massachusetts, he co-authored three books in addition to editing a collection of his father's wartime sermons.

49 Phillips Brooks, *Lectures on Preaching: Delivered Before the Divinity School of Yale College in January and February, 1877*. (New York: E. P. Dutton and Company, 60).

50 "Don Juan," by Lord George Gordon Byron, "The Confession of Harry Lorrequear Considered," in *Fraser's Magazine for Town and Country*, 22, (Sept. 1840), (London: James Fraser, 1840).

51 Original: "Other movements try to advance beyond their founders, but Christianity's slogan of advance has always been 'Back to Christ.'" From Sockman, *Recoveries in Religion*, 1938.

52 CM quotes from DPM's sermon, "Why Worry?" to illustrate his point "of a certain family during the war, who were in a desperate plight over the help situation. The certain family, as many people in our congregation suspected, was our family." *AMCP*, 181-82.

53 "Christianity Can Be Fun," *AMCP*, 128.

54 Original: "Neville Chamberlain, in one of his first speeches as new Prime Minister, likened the European situation to mountainous snow banks of hatred so poised that a voice might release and start an avalanche." Sockman, *Recoveries in Religion*, Cokesbury Press, 1938, 152.

55 Adolf Hitler (1889-1945), Chancellor of Germany (1933-1945)

56 Mary Brent Whiteside (1876-1962), "Who Has known Heights," in *The Eternal Quest*, (London: Erskine and MacDonald Company, 1926), originally published in *Harper's Magazine*.

57 "If there is anything that creates a peculiar passion, it is truth. It generates its own white heat. And if you preach what you believe, as if you believed it, as if it meant everything to you, there will be a natural ring and passion in your word that is infinitely better than any extraneous type of eloquence .... Truth is the one thing in every age and

station that has set the heather on fire. It has led martyrs to the stake with shining eyes, and turned the world upside down. I can't understand a man, speaking of a topic that concerns his own soul and the salvation of man, preaching with casualness or insipidity. If only he is in earnest and speaks as if he believes, there will be a ring even in his voice that will command and arrest. Please do not be ashamed of the enthusiasm that truth generates. All the great ages of history have been ages of enthusiasm, drunk with dreams. It was sheer enthusiasm that built and held the early Church, the passion of high belief, truth held so dear that as compared with it life was cheap." James Black, *The Mystery of Preaching,* (New York: Fleming H. Revell, 1924).

[58] Black, Ibid.

[59] DPM frequently preached "A Tap on the Shoulder," a sermon recounting his call to the ministry.

[60] Romans 12:3

[61] DPM knew personally about dangerous consequences. His Cape Cod neighbor and Washington ministerial colleague, the Very Rev. ZeBarney Thorne Phillips, rector of The Church of the Epiphany and U.S. Senate Chaplain (1927-1942), had been Dean of Washington National Cathedral for only seven months when, in May 1942, a pharmacist's error in compounding a prescription resulted in Phillips's sudden death.

[62] CM, *AMCP*, 206.

[63] 2 Samuel 12:5-6

[64] 2 Samuel 12:7

[65] Black, 60-61.

[66] George A. Buttrick, *Jesus Came Preaching: Christian Preaching in the New Age* (New York: Charles Scribner's Sons, 1936), 149.

[67] Richard Watson Gilder, "How to the Singer Comes the Song?" *The Century* 49, no. 2 (Dec., 1894), 202.

[68] DPM is indebted here to the ideas and language of Black, 45-46.

[69] "The dinner-table conversation in our home on any Wednesday night was likely to be the Sunday morning sermon. That was because the church bulletin went to press on Thursday. Invariably Peter would interrupt this sermon colloquy with, 'But what shall I *call* it?' There the sermon languished until the right title was forthcoming. By Thursday morning he might not know precisely what was going to be in the body of the sermon, but if he had a good title, he was happy. A flare for memorable titles was one facet of his gift for clipped and pungent phraseology." CM, *AMCP*, 198.

[70] Ibid. "Every Saturday night he methodically read and evaluated 'the agony columns,' as he called them, the church pages with the sermon topics of all the preachers."

[71] The Rev. Dr. Bernard C. Clausen (1875-1962) was the flamboyant pastor of First Baptist Church in Syracuse and First Baptist Church in Pittsburgh.

[72] DPM makes a passing reference to Robert Browning's "Home-Thoughts, from Abroad," written during a visit to Italy in 1845, and first published in his *Dramatic Romances and Lyrics.*

73 Black, 45.

74 Black, 46.

75 "Trying to 'get down deep' and answer the real questions of real men and women … was the ideal Peter had set for himself …. It resulted in wartime sermons like 'A Mother's Question' and 'God in Wartime,' dealing with the problem of why a loving God allows war; in 'how-to-do' sermons like 'Where Do I Begin?', 'Steps toward God,' 'The Wandering Sheep of Prayer'; in sermons like 'Christ and Sex' and 'Mr. Jones, Meet Jesus'—the latter on social drinking." CM, *AMCP*, 206.

76 Original: "And if you preach what you believe, as if you believed it, as if it meant everything to you, there will be a natural ring and passion in your word that is infinitely better than any extraneous type of eloquence." Black, 47.

77 The Augsburg Confession, one of the key documents of the Lutheran Reformation, holds the core beliefs of the Lutheran Church.

78 The Westminster Confession, originally drawn up by the 1646 Westminster Assembly as the confession of faith of the Church of England, underwent several revisions before being adopted in 1929 by the Synod of Philadelphia. It thus became *The Confession of our Faith and Larger and Shorter Catechisms* for the Presbyterian Church in the United States. With other revisions in 1787, 1861, and 1910, it remains the Church's doctrinal standard. DPM's copy is thoroughly underlined, studied, and many annotations written is the margins."

79 In his 1948 Lincoln, Lectures, DPM substituted Stalin for Hitler.

80 Martin Niemöller - see Lecture One, fn 61.

81 Eivind Berggrav - see Lecture One, fn. 60.

82 On February 1, 1942, a group of Quisling sympathizers in Trondheim invaded Nidaros Cathedral, Norway's Westminster Abbey. By day's end, they refused the cathedral dean entry to conduct services. Thousands of Norwegians gathered outside to sing "Ein' feste Burg ist unser Gott" (A mighty fortress is our God). The following day all seven Norwegian bishops resigned. Berggrav remained under house arrest for three years.

83 The Apostles Creed is a statement of faith in many Christian denominations.

84 "The earth has been so shrunk by the airplane and the radio that Europe is closer to America today than was one side of these [Great Smoky Mountains National Park] to the other side when the pioneers toiled through the primeval forest." Franklin D. Roosevelt, Address at Dedication of Great Smoky Mountains National Park, September 2, 1940. http://www.presidency.ucsb.edu/ws/?pid=16002 accessed October 15, 2014.

85 DPM's use of the terms "Negro" and "Jap" is consistent with the times in which this Lecture was delivered in 1944 and in 1948.

86 For his 1948 Lincoln Lectures, DPM deleted this and the next two paragraphs, no doubt in light of post-war revelations regarding the Chiang Kai-sheks.

87 Frigidaire, a brand founded in 1919, became synonymous with the generic "refrigerator."

88 "The organization of many appropriately called 'the Church of the Holy Refrigerator' is not inviting sinners to Christ ….You have been in churches … faultily splendid …

and splendidly nil," quoting "Faultily faultless, icily regular, splendidly null," by Alfred, Lord Tennyson in *Maud; A Monodrama*, 1855. Part I, section ii. Abraham Godchalk, *Godchalk Family History* (Harrisburg, Pa.: The United Evangelical Press, 1912), 222.

89 "For God so loved the world, that he gave his only begotten Son, that whosoever believeth in him should not perish, but have everlasting life."

90 Irwin Edman, *Adam, The Baby, and the Man from Mars* (Cambridge: Houghton Mifflin Co., 1929), 198. Quoted in Sockman, 144.

91 Charles Edward Montague, *Rough Justice* (Garden City, N Y.: Doubleday, Paige, and Company, 1926), 42ff. DPM also used a paraphrase of the "Little Bron" story in his sermon "Get Out of Step," *John Doe, Disciple* (New York: Fleming H. Revell, 1964) 94-95. This is an example of DPM's book sermon method.

92 A portion of this paraphrase appeared in *The Universalist Leader*, 121, Issue 42 (Boston: Universalist Publishing House, 1939).

93 DPM was probably referring to *Life* magazine. In December 1948, less than a month before his death, *Life* sent a photographer to cover his preaching mission in Neosho, Missouri, which had been postponed from June 1948, when DPM had suffered his second heart attack.

94 John 15:16

95 See CM, *AMCP*, 202.

96 John 15:5

97 I Corinthians 1:21

98 James Hastings and Edward Hastings, eds., *Speaker's Bible* (Aberdeen, Scotland: The Speaker's Bible Office, 1923-51, 1939) 30, 171.

99 American historian and novelist, Shelby Foote (1916-2005), said "the purpose of writing is to make people see."

100 A passing reference to line 49 ("Clung to the whistling mane of every wind") in the "Hound of Heaven," by Francis Thompson (1859–1907).

101 George Bernard Shaw (1856-1950), *Saint Joan: A Chronicle Play in Six Scenes and an Epilogue*, Scene I (London: Constable & Co., Ltd, 1924). He won the 1925 Nobel Prize in Literature.

102 Luke 10:26

103 Luke 10:27

104 Luke 10:28

105 Luke 10:29

106 Luke 10:37

107 DPM's pictorial illustration of Moses also appears in his sermon, "Compromise in Egypt," preached at NYAPC on February 20, 1944.

108 Exodus 5:1

109 DPM used this pictorial illustration in "Letters in the Sand," preached on January 23,

1938, and published in *AMCP*, 310-317. It also appears in "Broken Things," preached at NYAPC on March 22, 1942. DPM is heavily indebted for the ideas and phraseology of this vignette to Fulton J. Sheen, *The Eternal Galilean* (New York: D. Appleton-Century Company, Inc., 1934).

[110] John 8:5

[111] John 8:7

[112] Ibid.

[113] John 8:10

[114] John 8:11

[115] Ibid.

[116] DPM quotes nearly verbatim from Sheen, Ibid, 70, whose original is indented and enclosed in quotation marks but has no source citation. Extensive research has not revealed Sheen's source.

[117] Luke 19:2

[118] DPM first used this pictorial illustration of Zacchaeus in "The Disciple Up a Tree," during a preaching mission at St. Charles Presbyterian Church in New Orleans, February 22, 1940, and again in "A Tip or a Tithe," a sermon preached at NYAPC on February 24, 1946.

[119] While a student at Columbia Theological Seminary, DPM "listened intently to a sentence which he would remember for the rest of his life. 'Gentlemen,' the professor was saying, 'in writing your sermons, I beg of you, use a *sanctified imagination*.' … That was to become the keynote of Peter's preaching, his own peculiar contribution to the art of sermon making. Whereas most ministers write a sermon to develop an idea, Peter wrote his sermons to paint a picture and to arouse an emotion." CM, *AMCP*, 201.

[120] Matthew 10:22-23

[121] I Corinthians 11:24

[122] Matthew 6:27

[123] Black, *Mysteries of Preaching*, 154.

[124] Ibid.

[125] CM quotes this passage in "Preacher's Workshop," *AMCP*, 192-93.

[126] Buttrick, *Jesus Came Preaching*, 160. Here, Buttrick references Polonius to Laertes in Shakespeare, *Hamlet*, I, 3, 62-3: "Those Friends thou hast, and their adoption tried. *Grapple them unto thy soul with hooks of steel.*"

[127] "Lincoln's average word is a scant four letters long. Over 200 of his 272 words are just one syllable long. Over 250 are no longer than two syllables." A. E. Elmore, *Lincoln's Gettysburg Address: Echoes of the Bible and Book of Common Prayer* (Carbondale, Ill: Southern Illinois University Press, 2009) 96. *See also*, "Take the famous Gettysburg speech of Lincoln, and you will find what a marvelously plastic thing Anglo-Saxon English can be. Make such simple speaking your model, and your speech will become like words on wheels." Black, 117.

[128] For these suggestions, DPM is indebted to Buttrick, *Jesus Came Preaching*, 160.

[129] John Ruskin, *Modern Painters* (London: John Wiley and Sons, 1890), III, part iv, chap. 16, § 28, cited in Buttrick, 155.

[130] 2 Timothy 2:15

[131] Westminster Confession of Faith of 1646 with American Revision of 1789: "all [Scripture] which are given by inspiration of God to be the rule for faith and practice," 12, and "the infallible rule of interpretation of Scripture is the Scripture itself," 17.

[132] Hebrews 4:12

[133] "Q.3. *What do the Scriptures principally teach?* The Scriptures principally teach, what man is to believe concerning God, and what duty God requires of man." *Confession of Faith*, 376

[134] DPM used this material again in "Research Unlimited," preached on January 18, 1948, and at Boston's Old South Church on July 24, 1948.

[135] Galatians 6:2

[136] DPM wrote these Greek words by hand — βάρη (bareh) and φορτίον (phortion)—in blank spaces left by his secretaries.

[137] Genesis 2:7a

[138] By "English version," DPM refers to the King James Bible.

[139] DPM used this chemical elements illustration in "Rendezvous in Samarra," preached at the U.S. Naval Academy on the morning of December 7, 1941.

[140] Genesis 2:7bc

[141] *Oriental* (from the Latin *oriens,* meaning "rising") refers to the east; *occidental* (from the Latin *occidens,* meaning "setting") refers to the west as reckoned in relationship to Europe.

[142] DPM's use of *occidental* and *oriental* reminds his listeners that the writers of the Scriptures, coming from the Middle East (or Orient) approached their spirituality differently from the rational, scholastic philosophical tradition of westerners in the interpretation of Scripture.

[143] Ernest Taylor "Ernie" Pyle (1900–1945), a beloved American journalist who won the 1944 Pulitzer Prize for distinguished war correspondents, was killed in combat on April 18, 1945, six days after FDR died.

[144] *Eisegesis* is the reading of one's own ideas into the interpretation of a text, according to Andrew M. Denny, *Decoding Precepts of Oneness Theology* (Bloomington, Ind.: Westbow Press, 2018).

[145] Nero Claudius Caesar Augustus Germanicus (37-68 AD) ruling as Roman emperor from 54-68 AD.

[146] Titus Flavius Domitianus (51-96 AD) ruling as Roman emperor from 81-96 AD.

[147] Patmos is a small Greek island in the Aegean Sea, amongst the Dodecanese islands.

148 For his 1948 Lincoln Lectures, DPM substituted the phrase "behind the Iron Curtain" for "Nazi-occupied country." Winston Churchill gave his famous Iron Curtain speech on March 5, 1946, in Fulton, Missouri.

149 DPM use of the term "oriental" refers to the Middle East.

150 For his 1948 Lincoln Lectures, DPM changed "Stalin," leader of the Soviet Union, to "Hirohito," the emperor of Japan, who renounced his quasi-divine status after World War II.

151 DPM graduated from Columbia Theological Seminary, May 20, 1931.

152 Matthew 10:34

153 Mark 16:18

154 Diana was the Roman goddess of nature, fertility, and childbirth; Magna Mater ("Great Mother") cult is among the oldest religions in the world, dating to at least 6,000 before Christ's birth.

155 I Corinthians 8:13

156 DPM added the final four lines in his own hand.

157 When preparing Lecture V for publication—the only one previously published—DPM annotated the title page: "One of a series of lectures delivered at Gettysburg Seminary under the Zimmerman Foundation in May 1944." *Religion in Life*, 14, no. 2 (Spring, 1945), 195-204.

158 Quotation: "It revolutionized worship: the central place, which had been taken by the Mass, was claimed for the reading and preaching of the Word in a context of prayer." Fn: "This is expressed in the Ordination Service of the Church of England in which the priest receives into his hands, not a chalice, but a Bible." Frank Cairns, *The Prophet of the Heart, Being the Warrack Lectures on Preaching for 1934* (New York and London: Harper & Brothers Publishers, 1935), 37-38, quoting William P. Paterson (1860-1939), *The Rule of Faith* (London: Hodder and Stoughton, 1912), 278.

159 I Corinthians 2:1-4 *passim*.

160 "Peter was grateful that folks enjoyed hearing him preach but he strenuously objected when anyone referred to the rest of a service as "the preliminaries." For him, every word spoken in a service—the Invocation, the Offertory invitation, the hymns, the Scripture reading— was terribly important." CM, *AMCP*, 132.

161 DPM's extensive reliance on Cairns is reflected in his paraphrases and direct quote: "Such people have only one criterion for determining the value of the public worship of God, and that is the quality of the sermon. Everything up to the sermon is regarded as the 'preliminaries.'" Cairns, 33.

162 James Denney (1856-1917) from Cairns, 42, quoting from *The Way Everlasting: Sermons by James Denney* (London: Hodder and Stoughton, 1911), 104-105.

163 Acts 17:22-31

164 "And with the morn those angel faces smile, which I have loved long since, and lost awhile!" is the third stanza of *Lead, Kindly Light* by John Henry Newman (1801–1890).

This would have needed no further identification to an audience of seminarians in 1944 or clergy in 1948.

[165] NYAPC's original organ was built by John Brown in 1873; it was rebuilt into a new instrument by E. M. Skinner in 1942, with 23 stops added ten years later by Aeolian-Skinner. In 2009, A. E. Schleuter Pipe Organ Company of Lithonia, Georgia, installed a new three-manual instrument of 67 ranks, retaining 12 ranks of restored pipes from the Skinner and 1873 organs. See Cecelia H. Porter and Douglas R. Porter, "Music at NYAPC: In the Service of the Lord," in *Capital Witness: A History of The New York Avenue Presbyterian Church in Washington, D.C.,* (Franklin, Tenn., Plumbline Media, 2011), 356-378.

[166] The Celtic Cross mounted on the façade of the organ pipes in NYAPC is a hammered brass copy of the eighth- or ninth-century St. John's Cross, which once stood outside Iona Abbey on the Isle of Iona in Scotland's Inner Hebrides. The St. John's Cross replica was given to NYAPC by the Peter Marshall Scottish Memorial Committee in his memory. In 1949, this Committee published *The Exile Heart*, ten sermons and addresses by DPM before the Saint Andrew's Society of Washington for which he was their first chaplain, then president from 1941 until his death. The book's proceeds underwrote the Celtic Cross, DPM's tombstone at Fort Lincoln Cemetery, and endowed the Peter Marshall Professorship of Homiletics at Columbia Theological Seminary.

[167] CM included this sermon illustration in her *AMCP* account of falling in love with Peter while a student at Agnes Scott College from 1932 to 1936.

[168] DPM quotes, almost verbatim, passages from Black, *The Mystery of Preaching*, 167-168.

[169] Matthew 18:20

[170] Mark 16:15 and Matthew 28:20

[171] Black, 169

[172] Genesis 28:16

[173] Paul Fishbaugh was organist when DPM came to NYAPC; Karlian Meyer served from 1943 to 1947; British child prodigy Ronald Arnatt (1930-2018) served from 1947 to 1948. William Watkins (1926-2004) came to NYAPC in 1948 until 1955. During his eight years there he collaborated with G. Donald Harrison and Joseph S. Whiteford in rebuilding the church's Skinner organ.

[174] Shortly after arriving at NYAPC, DPM brought Charles Dana Beaschler (1905-1994) from Atlanta. A graduate of Westminster Choir College, he was NYAPC's director of music from 1939 to 1951, organizing the church's 160-voice choir and 35-piece orchestra.

[175] Note DPM's use of "he or she," unusual for the time. NYAPC's then-organist was Karlian Meyer (1919-1990), onetime student of Virgil Fox at Peabody Conservatory. In 1947, she entered Union Theological Seminary School of Sacred Music in New York, then returned to Washington as organist and director of music at First Baptist Church in Washington, D.C.

[176] DPM's forward-looking views on the role of music in worship reflect unmistakably the influence of Beaschler and his alma mater, Westminster Choir College in Princeton, NJ, where DPM was twice commencement speaker (1944, 1947) alongside its founder, Dr. John Finley Williamson.

[177] Late in the nineteenth century, NYAPC replaced its choir with a paid quartet of singers. By the mid-1800s, choirs had become increasingly common in American churches ... and 'notoriously ill- behaved.'" Cecelia Porter, *Capital Witness*, 365.

[178] Eighty years later little has changed. According to a 2010 Presbyterian Hymnal survey, 50 percent or more of the churches sang eighty-five of the 605 hymns at least once in the past year, but 50 percent or more of the church did not sing over 400 of the hymns in the 1990 hymnal.

[179] Words: Martin Luther (1483-1546); trans. Frederick H. Hedge (1805-1890), tune: *Ein feste Burg*

[180] Words: Isaac Watts (1674-1748); tune: *Hamburg*, arr. Lowell Mason (1792-1872)

[181] Words: Charles Wesley (1707-1788); tune: *Hollingside*, arr. J. B. Dukes (1923-1876)

[182] Words: William C. Doane (1832-1913); tune: *Albany*, arr. by J. Albert Jeffrey (1855-1929)

[183] Words: A. M. Toplady (1740-1778); tune: *Toplady*, T. Hastings (1784-1872)

[184] Words: George Keith or Richard Keen; tune: *Montgomery*, arr. S. Jarvis, 1762)

[185] Words: John Henry Newman (1801-1890); tune: *Lux benigna*, arr. John B. Dykes (1823-1876)

[186] Words: Frank Mason North (1850-1935); tune: *Germany*, William Gardiner (1770-1853)

[187] Words: John Ellerton; tune (1826-1893); tune: *St. Clement*, C. C. Scholefield (1839-1904)

[188] Words: S. J. Stone (1839-1900); tune: *Aurelia*, Samuel Sebastian Wesley (1810-1876)

[189] Words: Sabine Baring-Gould (1834-1924); tune: *St. Gertrude*, arr. Arthur Sullivan (1842-1900)

[190] Words: Bernard of Clairvaux; tune: *Passion Chorale* (melody, Hans Leo Hassler, harm. J. S. Bach (1685-1750)

[191] Words: Harry Emerson Fosdick (1878-1969); tune: *Cwm Rhondda*, John Hughes (1873–1932)

[192] Words: Irish poem, tr. Mary E. Byrne (1880-1931) and Eleanor H. Hull (1860-1935); tune: *Slane*, Traditional Irish air from Joyce's *Old Irish Folk Music and Songs*, 1920.

[193] Words: Katharina von Schlegel (1697-1777); tune: *Finlandia*, Jean Sibelius (1865-1957).

[194] Words: James E. Rowe (1866-1933); tune: *Howard E. Smith* (1864-1918)

[195] Text and tune: Frances Ridley Havergal (1836-1879), 1874.

[196] Gettysburg is a Lutheran seminary; Johann Sebastian Bach was a Lutheran composer.

210 Wolfgang Amadeus Mozart (1756-1791) was the preeminent composer of the Classical Era. His Requiem and Grand Mass in C Minor are at the core of the Western canon of musical repertoire.

211 Gioachino Rossini (1792–1868) was an Italian composer of sacred music, songs, and 39 operas.

212 Felix Mendelssohn (1809-1847) was an early Romantic German composer of Jewish heritage who reintroduced the music of J. S. Bach to a new generation in 1827.

213 John Stainer (1840-1901), an English composer and organist at St Paul's Cathedral, London, is best remembered today for his cantata, *The Crucifixion*, popular during his lifetime.

214 Black, *The Mystery of Preaching*, 218-219.

215 Ibid, 219.

216 Romans 8:26

217 "Curb market" a list of securities for sale not listed on a stock exchange.

218 Matthew 6:24-33

219 John 14:1-14. In preparing this manuscript for publication by *Religion in Life*, op. cit., DPM deleted these two Scriptural passages. In the oral lecture, he could demonstrate with his voice inflections and gestures how to read Scripture, which cannot be conveyed on the printed page.

197 DPM crossed out "lungs" and wrote "throat," puzzling since proper singing t
requires breathing from the diaphragm rather than the throat.

198 "In 1900, NYAPC dismissed its choir and turned to a paid quartet of singers. *
the change caused some dissention, the quartet led congregational sing
performed anthems and solos during most services until 1939," writes Cecel
in *Capital Witness,* 361. That all changed on May 2, 1939, when the Session
institute the Westminster Choir College plan of graded choirs.

199 "On Friday morning, September 1st, [1944], Alma Deane Fuller, a Kansan, w
newspaper reporter on Capitol Hill, decided to join the choir of our church in
be sure of a seat at the morning service." CM, *AMCP,* 183.

200 Dudley Buck (1838-1909) was a Boston organist and composer whose works
four cantatas, fifty-five anthems, and twenty sacred songs, all labeled "mau
super-saccharine" by Leonard W. Ellinwood in his *History of American Chur*
(New York: Morehouse-Gorham Company, 1953), 115.

201 F. Melius Christiansen (1871-1955), a Norwegian native and choral conduct
Lutheran tradition, founded the famed St. Olaf College Choir, which he co
from 1912 to 1944.

202 Harry T. Burleigh (1866-1949) was an African American classical compo
famed baritone at St. George's Episcopal Church, New York.

203 Noble Cain (1896-1977) was the choral director at Northwestern University, a
the musical director at NBC Radio and a well-known composer of a cappella

204 Hugh S. Roberton (1874-1952), a Scottish composer, was Britain's leading
master in the first half of the twentieth century.

205 Clarence Dickinson (1873-1969) served as organist-choirmaster at Brick Presl
Church in New York City for over fifty years. He was founding director of the
Theological Seminary School of Sacred Music and a founder of The America
of Organists.

206 T. Tertius Noble (1867–1953), an Englishman, was organist and choirmaste
Cathedral (1892-1898) and York Minster (1898-1913). He immigrated to Am
establish a choral tradition along Anglican cathedral lines at St Thomas E
Church in New York City, where he founded the Choir School for Boys in 191

207 Ernest Krikor Emurian (1912-2004), son of an Armenian immigrant, was p
Cherrydale United Methodist Church in Arlington, Virginia and author of mo
sixty hymns.

208 Jean Sibelius (1865-1957) was a Finnish composer whose music played a key
creating a Finnish national identity.

209 Johann Sebastian Bach (1685-1750), a German Lutheran composer, and (
Frideric Handel (1685-1759), a German/English court composer, were the l
masters of the Baroque era. Only in the 1950s did the music of Bach and I
reemerge in the churches and concerts halls of America. NYAPC organist K
Meyer accompanied the Washington Choral Society in the first complete Washi
performance of Bach's *St. Matthew Passion* on April 13, 1943.

197 DPM crossed out "lungs" and wrote "throat," puzzling since proper singing technique requires breathing from the diaphragm rather than the throat.

198 "In 1900, NYAPC dismissed its choir and turned to a paid quartet of singers. Although the change caused some dissention, the quartet led congregational singing and performed anthems and solos during most services until 1939," writes Cecelia Porter in *Capital Witness,* 361. That all changed on May 2, 1939, when the Session voted to institute the Westminster Choir College plan of graded choirs.

199 "On Friday morning, September 1st, [1944], Alma Deane Fuller, a Kansan, who was a newspaper reporter on Capitol Hill, decided to join the choir of our church in order to be sure of a seat at the morning service." CM, *AMCP,* 183.

200 Dudley Buck (1838-1909) was a Boston organist and composer whose works include four cantatas, fifty-five anthems, and twenty sacred songs, all labeled "maudlin and super-saccharine" by Leonard W. Ellinwood in his *History of American Church Music* (New York: Morehouse-Gorham Company, 1953), 115.

201 F. Melius Christiansen (1871-1955), a Norwegian native and choral conductor in the Lutheran tradition, founded the famed St. Olaf College Choir, which he conducted from 1912 to 1944.

202 Harry T. Burleigh (1866-1949) was an African American classical composer and famed baritone at St. George's Episcopal Church, New York.

203 Noble Cain (1896-1977) was the choral director at Northwestern University, as well as the musical director at NBC Radio and a well-known composer of a cappella music.

204 Hugh S. Roberton (1874-1952), a Scottish composer, was Britain's leading choral master in the first half of the twentieth century.

205 Clarence Dickinson (1873-1969) served as organist-choirmaster at Brick Presbyterian Church in New York City for over fifty years. He was founding director of the Union Theological Seminary School of Sacred Music and a founder of The American Guild of Organists.

206 T. Tertius Noble (1867–1953), an Englishman, was organist and choirmaster at Ely Cathedral (1892-1898) and York Minster (1898-1913). He immigrated to America to establish a choral tradition along Anglican cathedral lines at St Thomas Episcopal Church in New York City, where he founded the Choir School for Boys in 1919.

207 Ernest Krikor Emurian (1912-2004), son of an Armenian immigrant, was pastor of Cherrydale United Methodist Church in Arlington, Virginia and author of more than sixty hymns.

208 Jean Sibelius (1865-1957) was a Finnish composer whose music played a key role in creating a Finnish national identity.

209 Johann Sebastian Bach (1685-1750), a German Lutheran composer, and George Frideric Handel (1685-1759), a German/English court composer, were the leading masters of the Baroque era. Only in the 1950s did the music of Bach and Handel reemerge in the churches and concerts halls of America. NYAPC organist Karlian Meyer accompanied the Washington Choral Society in the first complete Washington performance of Bach's *St. Matthew Passion* on April 13, 1943.

210 Wolfgang Amadeus Mozart (1756-1791) was the preeminent composer of the Classical Era. His Requiem and Grand Mass in C Minor are at the core of the Western canon of musical repertoire.

211 Gioachino Rossini (1792–1868) was an Italian composer of sacred music, songs, and 39 operas.

212 Felix Mendelssohn (1809-1847) was an early Romantic German composer of Jewish heritage who reintroduced the music of J. S. Bach to a new generation in 1827.

213 John Stainer (1840-1901), an English composer and organist at St Paul's Cathedral, London, is best remembered today for his cantata, *The Crucifixion*, popular during his lifetime.

214 Black, *The Mystery of Preaching*, 218-219.

215 Ibid, 219.

216 Romans 8:26

217 "Curb market" a list of securities for sale not listed on a stock exchange.

218 Matthew 6:24-33

219 John 14:1-14. In preparing this manuscript for publication by *Religion in Life,* op. cit., DPM deleted these two Scriptural passages. In the oral lecture, he could demonstrate with his voice inflections and gestures how to read Scripture, which cannot be conveyed on the printed page.